PRAISE FOR
RESILIENT ORGAN

'A truly excellent read on a key global topic that explores all of the critical ingredients in one easy-to-digest book. Erica Seville should be congratulated on making such a major contribution to the vital concept of resilient organizations.' **Peter Power, Chairman, World Conference on Disaster Management, and MD, Visor Consultants (UK) Ltd**

'This new book is impressive. Impressive because it shows how years of quality academic research can be turned into very useful, actionable knowledge that can impact and benefit organizations and in turn society.' **Eve Coles, Visiting Research Fellow, UK Cabinet Office EPC, Editor, *Emergency Management Review*, and Founder Member, Future City and Community Resilience Network**

'Erica Seville's *Resilient Organizations* is an extremely readable and practical distillation of the work done over the last decade by Resilient Organisations. Not a dry summary of research, the book is a 'how to' manual to help organizations become more resilient, peppered with examples to help understanding.' **John Plodinec, Community and Regional Resilience Institute**

'Not just a summary of the issues but a real *how to* anticipate and act to avoid where it is possible and to recover in the most business/socially effective ways.' **James B Porter, Jr, Chief Engineer and Vice President Engineering and Operations, DuPont (retired)**

'In 2009, in my role as co-leader of the University of Canterbury's emergency preparedness programme, when we needed to step our progress up a gear, we turned to Erica to assist us. From that point on she became both an ardent supporter and trusted confidant and when the 2010 and 2011 earthquakes devastated the city, Erica became a key member of our operations centre team. She has not only undertaken extensive research on the subjects contained in this book, she has lived and breathed their reality. I will be both using and widely sharing the insights Erica provides and this book will have pride of place on my bookshelf.' **Chris Hawker, Regional Manager and Group Controller, Emergency Management Otago**

'This book presents a comprehensive and practical road map to building a resilient organization that can survive and thrive in a world which is volatile, uncertain, complex and ambiguous.' **David Parsons, Adjunct Associate Professor, Queensland University of Technology – Centre for Emergency and Disaster Management, Australia**

'An outstanding guide to how to build deep resilience in real-life organizations. The chapter on Social Capital is really useful. I only wish it had been published before the Canterbury earthquakes started.' **Roger Sutton, former Chief Executive, Canterbury Earthquake Recovery Authority**

'Erica's excellent use of case studies brings to life organizational resilience in a meaningful and practical way to implement within any organization.' **Peter Brouggy, Co-Chair, Resilience Expert Advisory Group (REAG), Chair, BCI Australasia 2020 Group**

'I really enjoyed *Resilient Organizations*. I found it practical and easy to read, punctuated with real-life, unsanitized stores that are relevant and compelling. It struck me that four of the five most important elements of resilient organizations are all about people. Leadership, staff engagement, 3am friends and learning and innovation are fundamentally about human behaviour. This is refreshing. In the past, resilience has tended to be the domain of engineers and accountants. While those aspects are important, they only exist to support communities where they work, live and play. If the Christchurch experience has taught us anything, it is that people must be at the centre of everything resilient. *He tangata*. Organizations are fundamentally about people, and *Resilient Organizations* manages to make this point firmly but yet unobtrusively and compellingly. Great job.' **Mike Mendonça, Wellington Chief Resilience Officer**

'Erica Seville has unlocked the code on resilience. From natural disasters to market turbulence, she explains how any organization can learn to cope with disruption.' **Debbie van Opstal, Executive Director, US Resilience Project**

'There *is* some hidden advantage to living through 12,000 New Zealand earthquakes in two years after all. Erica's book integrates disaster stories, thoughtful analysis and simple practical steps into an eminently readable book that explains how – and why – resilience is a competitive advantage.' **Nathaniel Forbes, Singapore**

Resilient Organizations

Resilient Organizations

How to survive, thrive and create opportunities through crisis and change

Erica Seville

Kogan Page

LONDON PHILADELPHIA NEW DELHI

First published in Great Britain and the United States in 2017 by Kogan Page Limited

2nd Floor, 45 Gee Street	c/o Martin P Hill Consulting	4737/23 Ansari Road
London EC1V 3RS	122 W 27th Street	Daryaganj
United Kingdom	New York, NY 10001	New Delhi 110002
	USA	India

© Erica Seville 2017

The right of Erica Seville to be identified as the author of this work has been asserted by her in accordance with the Copyright, Designs and Patents Act 1988.

ISBN	978 0 7494 7855 1
E-ISBN	978 0 7494 7856 8

British Library Cataloguing-in-Publication Data

A CIP record for this book is available from the British Library.

Library of Congress Control Number
2016956896

Typeset by SPi Global
Print production managed by Jellyfish
Printed and bound in Great Britain by CPI Group (UK) Ltd, Croydon CR0 4YY

For Micah and Sam

CONTENTS

ABOUT THE AUTHOR

Erica is co-Leader of Resilient Organisations and Director of Resilient Organisations Ltd. Resilient Organisations is a public-good research programme involving a team of over 35 researchers, working collaboratively to improve the resilience of organizations so they can both survive adversity and thrive in a world of uncertainty. Resilient Organisations Ltd involves a small and vibrant group of people doing research and consulting, working directly with organizations to help them find the best ways to improve their resilience.

A leading researcher in the field of organizational resilience, Erica has authored over 100 research articles and is a regular international speaker on resilience. Erica is a member of the leadership team, and leads the Pathways to Resilience Flagship within QuakeCoRE, the New Zealand Centre of Research Excellence dedicated to improving earthquake resilience. She is also a member of the Resilience Expert Advisory Group (REAG), providing advice and support to the Australian Federal Government on organizational resilience issues. Erica is an Adjunct Senior Fellow with the Department of Civil and Natural Resources Engineering at the University of Canterbury and has a PhD in risk management.

When not working, Erica fills her time looking after two growing boys, together with her husband Richard, in rural Canterbury, New Zealand.

ACKNOWLEDGEMENTS

This book is the culmination of more than a decade's worth of research by the Resilient Organisations community of researchers. They are such a fantastic group of people to work with – enthusiastic, curious, motivated, collaborative and brilliant – thanks team!

To find out more about Resilient Organisations, visit our website www. resorgs.org.nz

The case for resilience

Swiss Air was once one of the most admired airlines in the world. Famous for its punctuality and superior service, it was also considered to be so financially stable that it was nicknamed 'the flying bank'.

But that all changed.

Not long after the 11 September 2001 terror attacks, Swiss Air's planes were suddenly grounded on tarmacs around the world.[1] Forty thousand passengers were stranded and hundreds of staff made jobless. There wasn't enough cash to pay for fuel or landing fees. Swiss Air had run out of money.

What led to this spectacular collapse of a once highly successful and stable organization? The 11 September terror attacks created unprecedented disruption to the aviation industry – but although this may have been the trigger for Swiss Air's demise, it certainly wasn't the cause.

Problems for Swiss Air started in the late 1990s, when the airline board decided to follow an aggressive borrowing and acquisition policy called the 'Hunter Strategy'. As a mid-sized carrier, Swiss Air had found that it was neither big enough to be a market leader nor small enough to fit into a niche. Based in Switzerland, the airline had high operating costs, and, because Switzerland is not a member of the European Union, Swiss Air did not have the freedom to expand alone across Europe. Swiss Air started looking for solutions. Initially it started joining global alliances, but after a few years decided to try another strategy – buying stakes in a string of other European airlines.

Swiss Air had leveraged itself up with debt, and the airlines it had purchased weren't performing well. Its survival was in the balance – and then the 11 September attacks occurred. As disruption rippled through the aviation industry, Swiss Air recorded losses of CHF 65 million (USD 41m) in just 10 days.[2] Swissair simply couldn't handle the hit – the 'flying bank' was all out of cash. Over the course of a decade, the company had gone from a source of national pride to notoriety as one of the most spectacular corporate collapses. Was this a case of bad luck or bad management? In its attempts to deal with one set of problems, Swiss Air had reduced its ability to deal with shock events. It had failed to manage its resilience as a strategic asset.

So often when we think about resilience, we think of the moment of crisis. But resilience comes from deeper within an organization's history. Over many years, Swiss Air had developed a culture and style of management that effectively prevented discussion of differences. One past employee described how everything was fine as long as your opinion remained the same as that of the group. Challenging the mainstream thinking with different views was almost impossible.

Ineffective and suboptimal group decision making negatively affected the health of Swiss Air and, ultimately, its resilience. For Swiss Air, it may have been the disruption following the 11 September attacks that tipped the company over the edge, but the culture it had developed over the previous decade had led the organization to the cliff's edge.

Over the past decade, I have co-led Resilient Organisations,[3] a public-good research programme based in New Zealand. Together with John Vargo and a team of 35 fantastic researchers, we seek to understand what helps and hinders an organization's resilience. For 12 years, our research has focused on organizations of all shapes and sizes. We have discovered that, whether an organization is a large multinational, a small business, a government agency, a charity, a sports club or a co-operative, the principles of organizational resilience remain the same.

Within the research community, excitement is building. We are starting to unlock the mysteries as to what enables some organizations to thrive in the face of adversity, while others wilt and fail. We have managed to identify a suite of leading indicators that can diagnose how resilient an organization is likely to be in the face of future crises, and have also developed tools for measuring and monitoring levels of resilience over time.

There is still a long way to go to build a complete picture of what drives an organization's resilience, but the good news is that we now know that any organization can become more resilient if it wants to. In this book I will translate for you what the latest research is telling us about what makes organizations resilient, turning it into tangible, practical advice that you can implement in your own organization, starting today.

Becoming future-ready

All organizations go through natural business cycles. The one certainty is that at some time during its life, every organization is likely to face a disruptive crisis. Be it a natural disaster, a reputational crisis, problems within the supply chain or an issue affecting its people, organizational crises happen more often than we think.

In the late 1990s, Deborah Pretty from Oxford Metrica started looking at the frequency of crises striking large corporations.[4] Taking five years' worth of share price data on the largest 1,000 companies in the world, she analysed the percentage that experienced a crisis severe enough to cause a sudden fall in their share price. Looking for share prices that fell by 30 per cent or more within a month, her findings were staggering. More than 40 per cent of the world's largest companies had experienced such a crisis within just five years. One of our researchers, Amy Stephenson,[5] surveyed businesses in Auckland, New Zealand and found similarly high rates of crises, with 41 per cent of organizations reporting that they had experienced a crisis within the last five years.

Many people seem to think that crises are rare events, but they are not. If your organization has a 40 per cent chance of experiencing a crisis sometime in the next five years, shouldn't you take the resilience of your organization seriously?

Crises impact organizations on a daily basis. In just 10 years, for example, one firm I know experienced four very different crises: a major employment dispute; power struggles within the leadership team for strategic control; damage to its premises requiring sudden and permanent evacuation; and then the breakaway of a group of staff to set up a rival firm. This firm's experience is not an outlier and these types of event are not unusual – they are happening to organizations every day. If handled poorly, they have the ability to bring an organization to its knees.

But change and disruption are not always negative – they can also be invigorating for an organization. Renewal can bring the injection of new skills and perspectives. Existential crises can lead to an organization re-evaluating its goals, taking a fresh look at its operating environment and finding new opportunities to explore.

Our challenge for the 21st century is to create organizations that are future-ready, with an inbuilt capacity not only to weather the storms of change, but to be able to thrive in such environments. We need organizations that proactively identify and manage the risks that can be anticipated, but also invest in capabilities to cope with events that cannot be anticipated. We need organizations that are capable of sensing changes in their operating environment, can quickly grasp the implications of those changes for their organization, and are agile and strategic in their response. These will be the organizations that thrive in the rapidly changing environments of the future.

It is possible to proactively develop such a resilience capability within any organization.

The time for change

In March 2000, lightning struck a high-voltage line in New Mexico, causing a fire at the Royal Philips Electronics manufacturing plant.[6] The fire was relatively minor – and was put out in just 10 minutes. The problem wasn't the fire itself so much as the smoke and dust generated while putting out the fire. Computer chips don't tend to like getting dirty. The smoke and dust had just contaminated a stockpile of product waiting to be shipped – millions of tiny computer chips for use in mobile phones.

At the time, Phillips had two very high-profile customers for its computer chips – Nokia and arch-rival Ericsson. Phillips surveyed the damage and initially estimated that production would be restored within a week. Nokia and Ericsson responded very differently to this information.

Nokia, understanding the vulnerability it had to any production delays, and dubious about how long it might take for the Phillips plant to actually get back into production, proactively began to work with Phillips to find workarounds. Together they redesigned the chips used in Nokia phones to enable them to be manufactured at other Phillips plants.

Ericsson, on the other hand, was much slower to respond. Taking the estimated restoration time at face value, it appears that Ericsson did little 'just-in-case' planning. No such alternative options were developed.

It took a full six weeks before production finally restarted at the Phillips factory, and by that time Ericsson had a major problem on its hands. It had a critical shortage of chips for its phones, and the fleeter-of-foot Nokia had already secured all of the additional capacity in the market.

With about 7 million phones affected by supply and quality issues, Ericsson's sales and margins dropped, inventories increased and cost went up owing to production lines lying idle. By the middle of the year, Ericsson reported that the fire had caused a second-quarter operating loss of $200 million in its mobile phone division.[7] Nokia, on the other hand, reported that its third-quarter profits had risen by 42 per cent.[8] A relatively minor fire, and their response to it, had caused a divergence in the two companies' fortunes – a divergence from which Ericsson never really recovered.

Think for a moment: if faced with a critical supply disruption, would your organization be a Nokia or an Ericsson? How has your organization responded to past disruptions? Did it approach them proactively? Did it manage to find an upside from the challenge?

The story of Nokia and Ericsson has been around for many years in the resilience world, ever since it was highlighted by Yossi Sheffi in his great book *The Resilient Enterprise*.[9] There is an interesting sequel to this story, however. It is worth bearing in mind that resilience is both dynamic and contextual.

Resilience is dynamic because it changes over time. An organization that was once resilient can have its resilience eroded over time if it doesn't keep its eye on the ball. Resilience is also contextual – every organization has its particular weaknesses. One of our researchers, Venkataraman Nilakant, points out that while Nokia was very adept at managing the operational crisis created by the fire, it then failed dismally at responding to the strategic challenge of shifting customer demand towards smartphones.

The research journey to discover resilience indicators

In 2005, a tornado ripped through Greymouth, a small town on the West Coast of New Zealand. The tornado cut a path through an industrial area of town – over the top of an engineering firm called Dispatch and Garlick. Hearing the tornado coming, staff quickly ran for cover. As they sheltered under the work benches, whole sections of the roof were torn away from the factory. It was incredible that no one was hurt.

Dispatch and Garlick now had a real problem. It had been working hard to fill an international order for an important client – it was due to be shipped the following week. How could the firm possibly achieve that now?

Dave McMillian is the owner of Dispatch and Garlick. At the time of the tornado, Dave was three hours from the factory, at his father's funeral. Getting a call to say that a tornado had just torn the roof off his factory was the last thing he needed. He immediately returned to Greymouth to help coordinate the recovery effort.

Then something special happened. The firm's team of about 50 staff pulled together, with a 'can-do' attitude and a very clear and united purpose of getting the factory back up and operating. The entire Greymouth community also rallied round the company in support. Even its competitors pitched in, providing resources, help and support. The staff were back, working to complete that customer order, the very next morning – working under tarpaulins in case of rain.

At the time of the tornado, our research group, Resilient Organisations, was just beginning to form. We had just won our first research funding to identify what helps and hinders organizations in becoming resilient. My husband is a structural engineer, and the following week he was called to Greymouth to take a look at the factory, which is a heritage building, to see how it could be saved and repaired. I decided to go along too, to find out some more about how the business was coping with this sudden crisis.

Upon arrival, I could see that the company was doing remarkably well. Only a week after the disaster, it had managed to ship its export order and the workplace had a surprising sense of calm confidence. I was amazed. Sitting down with Dave McMillan over a coffee, I started to ask him about how the company had managed to recover so quickly.

Coming from a background in risk management, and having worked in the banking sector in the UK, I was expecting to hear a story about how the company's business continuity plan or emergency response plan was activated. I soon discovered that the business had done little preparation for crises. It hadn't done any formal risk management, didn't have any type of plan for what to do in the event of a crisis – and yet this business had managed to come through such a catastrophic event remarkably well. This made me really start to wonder – what is it that gives some organizations the ability to rise to the challenge in times of adversity?

This was a Eureka moment. As researchers, it forced us to challenge our assumption that the way to make organizations more resilient was to get them to plan and prepare for crisis in better and more comprehensive ways. Instead, we began to wonder if there might be something about the organizations themselves, their character, their ethos, their ways of operating, that made them more, or less, resilient.

We decided to set our prior assumptions aside and embarked on a grounded theory approach to discover what leads to resilience in an organization.

We did this by examining, in depth, the resilience of 10 very different organizations.[10] We purposefully selected organizations of different sizes, with different ownership structures and operating in different sectors. Some of our case study organizations had recent crisis experience, others didn't. Our case studies included a multinational corporation, a small family-run IT company, an infrastructure organization listed on the stock exchange, a nationwide construction contracting firm, a rural local government organization, a large co-operative, a tertiary institution, a government-owned critical infrastructure provider and a supermarket. One of our PhD students, Sonia McManus, then spent the next three years getting to know these 10 organizations very well. She interviewed people throughout each organization, to understand how the organization operated in its day-to-day environment, how the organization was positioned to respond to crises, how it had responded to past crises, and the suite of capabilities and competencies the organization had to draw on if needed.

Each of the organizations had its own nuances and character – but what we were looking for were those things that emerged that weren't tied to a particular industry sector, type of production process or geographic location. We were seeking out those things that underpin the resilience of *any* organization.

Through Sonia's research we came up with our very first suite of resilience indicators. Over the years we have stress-tested those indicators with many other cohorts of organizations. Although there have been refinements made, in essence the early ideas that emerged from Sonia's initial research have remained true – that resilience emerges from an organization's culture; that it isn't just *what* an organization does that is important, but *how* it goes about doing it that leads to resilience.

Along that journey we also discovered some important insights that have helped to shape our thinking. The first is that organizations can become myopic when thinking about the types of crisis that might befall them. It surprised us how many organizations were fixated on being better prepared for the last crisis that had struck them. If they had recently experienced a flood, for example, flooding risk was the only thing they could talk about.

We also found that some organizations had pigeon-holed resilience as being only relevant in times of crisis. Few were seeing the link between their organization's ability to deal with large-scale disruption and their ability to cope with the ups and downs of everyday business.

We also struck a really interesting phenomenon in which public sector organizations struggled to visualize what 'organizational failure' might look like for their organization. They were so locked into thinking of failure in terms of 'financial failure' or 'going out of business' (something that doesn't tend to happen if you are a government-backed entity) that we had to work hard to show the relevance of resilience for them.

These insights highlighted the need to seek out resilience capabilities that would not just help organizations survive sudden shock events, but actually help them thrive in everyday business. They challenged us to develop resilience strategies that would help organizations cope with any kind of adversity, whether it was perceived as a significant risk or not. They also pushed us to conceptualize resilience as more than just financial survival – as a capability to continue delivering on an organization's core objectives (those things to which it holds most dear), no matter what the situation.

Recognizing resilience in your organization

There is no one formula for how to design a perfectly resilient organization. Different aspects can either enhance or erode an organization's resilience, depending on how they are managed. There are, however, indicators of resilience that organizations can proactively foster.

An organization's resilience is drawn from both its planned and adaptive capabilities. Organizations that invest in their planned resilience capabilities are able to sense change as it emerges over the horizon, and take action both to minimize the downside risk and to extract maximum upside. They are able to prevent many crises from ever occurring, and when crises do occur, they are able to manage them responsively and effectively.

But planned resilience capabilities will only get an organization so far. No crisis ever fits the plan, and organizations inevitably need to find ways to adapt and evolve. Being *both* planned and adaptive – this is the key to resilience (Figure 1.1).

Figure 1.1 Resilience requires both planned and adaptive capabilities

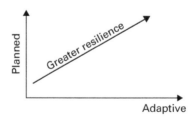

Many organizations that are weak on planning will often try to rely on their adaptive capabilities to get them out of trouble. In New Zealand, we have a

saying that captures this attitude perfectly – 'She'll be right, mate!' But a 'She'll be right' approach can lead to a siege mentality – where an organization is constantly fighting fires and dealing with crises that could have easily been averted if some basic planning had been in place. It is far better for an organization to be proactive in preventing the crisis from occurring in the first place.

As resilience researchers, we are often asked if any particular type of organization is fundamentally more resilient than others. We have found that being resilient isn't the preserve of a certain 'type' of organization. Any organization, regardless of size or structure, can build planned and adaptive resilience capabilities. All types of organization can also be hotbeds of dysfunction.

Resilience doesn't directly correlate to the amount of resources an organization has; it relates more to how an organization can access and utilize resources when it needs them. For example, large multinational corporations can be resilient, drawing from their large pool of resources. But they can also suffer from being less responsive and agile. Small businesses have fewer resources under their direct control, but if they are well networked and connected with other organizations, they can access a large pool of resources when they need it.

Similarly, different organizational structures can either support or erode resilience, depending on how they are implemented. Organizations that are very hierarchical can be highly resilient when there is a strong leadership team in place. But a hierarchical organization can suffer if leaders become disconnected from those they are leading (ie the leaders don't have willing followers). We regularly find that resilience is less dependent on the structural design of the organization than it is on the relationship between the people and groups within that organization.

Organizations operating in different sectors face different resilience challenges, but none is fundamentally destined to be more, or less, resilient than another. Organizations in highly regulated environments can sometimes find themselves constrained in their ability to innovate and implement novel solutions at short notice. Organizations operating in highly competitive environments may have more incentive to innovate, but also have a customer base that will very quickly switch allegiances at the first hint of failure.

And it isn't just for-profit organizations that need to become resilient. Other types of organization face similar hurdles.

Ever heard of Livestrong? This not-for-profit organization was formerly known as the Lance Armstrong Foundation. It had to rebrand in the wake of Armstrong eventually admitting to doping during his Tour de France campaigns. The Foundation's finances were once boosted by sales of millions of yellow bracelets, and they had the ability to attract thousands of people to celebrity cycling events. After Armstrong's admission, Nike ended its lucrative sponsorship deal for the distinctive yellow bracelets. The Foundation has had to find ways to retain its identity while distancing itself from its charismatic founder. Time will tell how it manages these challenges. As CEO Doug Ulman says: '[Livestrong is] never going to be the same. In the future, could it be better? It could be'.[11]

Government organizations also need resilience. The city of Detroit is just one of many examples around the world of cities struggling back from bankruptcy. Detroit's problems were more of the 'slow-burn' kind of adversity rather than a single cataclysmic event, but the resulting crisis is just as severe. The city of Detroit relies on property taxes to provide public services, but property values dropped 77 per cent in real terms in the half-century since the 1960s.[12] As Detroit's industrial backbone, the automotive industry, went into decline, it left in its wake massive unemployment, uninviting cityscapes and contaminated land. The city faced falling population, degraded infrastructure and ultimately financial insolvency. With its recent declaration of bankruptcy, some are hoping that there is now the opportunity for the city of Detroit to start the process of recovery. The city will need the right leadership, culture and attitude to be able to bring about its own renewal.

What these examples illustrate is that resilience is not just an issue of concern for corporate entities. No matter what size, sector or type of organization you are with, the ideas in this book will help you to make your organization more resilient. There is no time like the present – start today.

Being alert to change

Feeling confident that your organization is already resilient? Great, use this book to test your assumptions and then make sure you keep your eye on the ball. Just because your organization is resilient today doesn't mean it will remain resilient tomorrow. As organizations go through normal changes, their level of resilience fluctuates. A prolonged period of stress can erode your organization's resilience as staff become fatigued and the organization is tempted to hunker down, taking a defensive position while it weathers the storm. Similarly, organizations going through restructuring inevitably lose skilled and experienced staff, along with the social capital and institutional memory that they hold, thus reducing your organization's resilience.

If everyday life can erode an organization's resilience, think what a massive earthquake can do to it. Many of the researchers from our team live in Christchurch, which in 2010 was struck by a magnitude 7.1 earthquake. The earthquake was centred just 40 km west of the city. Our team quickly started to capture how the earthquake had impacted organizations across the local region; our idea was to track these organizations throughout their recovery.

The study then got a whole lot more interesting. There wasn't just one earthquake. Over the next two years the city experienced over 12,000 earthquakes. The study shifted gear as we started monitoring a city full of organizations facing ongoing crisis.

In the Christchurch study, we collected data on how organizations scored against 13 indicators of resilience. We randomly selected organizations from seven slices across the Christchurch economy to survey.

Five of these slices related to particular sectors of the economy. We surveyed organizations in the building supplies sector, a sector likely to be critical to the rebuilding of the city. We also looked at organizations in the fast-moving consumer goods sector, which includes food producers, supermarkets and corner stores selling everyday items for the community. The third sector we looked at was ICT – the information, communications and technology sector. This sector is high-growth, critical to the regional economy. We also captured data from critical infrastructure providers that deliver electricity, water, sewage, telecommunications, transportation and so on – those services on which a community critically relies. The final sector we examined was trucking, which provides the logistical interface between many different parts of the economy through supply chains.

We also took two geographic slices through the economy, the first looking at organizations operating from Christchurch's Central Business District, and the second looking at organizations based in a neighbouring small town that was also badly damaged – the Kaiapoi Town Centre.

In Figure 1.2 you can see how the resilience of organizations within each of the sectors was faring in late 2010, just after the first earthquake hit. Most organizations were tracking reasonably well; they had come through the crisis with their resilience largely intact.

Little did we know at the time, but those data then served as an excellent baseline for understanding what happened next. Six months later, the city was struck again, by a 6.3 magnitude shake. Although the magnitude of this earthquake was smaller than the first earthquake, this time it was located right underneath the city and therefore much more devastating. Once the dust had settled, our team surveyed the same organizations again to see how they were faring. The results were stark, with a collapse in resilience across all sectors (Figure 1.3).

Figure 1.2 Resilience intact – resilience of organizations across different sectors of the Canterbury economy soon after the 4 September 2010 earthquake

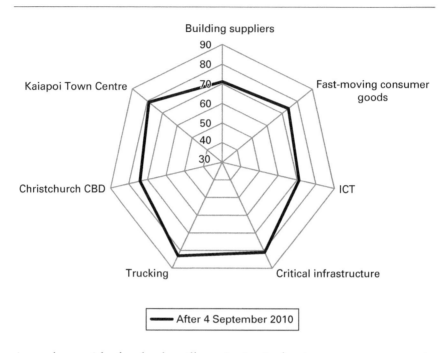

A year later, with aftershocks still continuing in the city, our team once again surveyed these same organizations to see how and if they were recovering (Figure 1.4).

Resilience had started to rebuild for many of the organizations, but not for all. Of particular note were organizations that had previously been located in the Christchurch Central Business District. One year on from the major earthquake, the Central Business District was still behind a cordon. Building owners, and some business owners, were allowed through the cordon with an escort, but, on the whole, the area was off-limits owing to the number of damaged and dangerous buildings. Many of these organizations were open and operating – but from temporary premises scattered across the city. With major uncertainty over when or if they would be able to reopen back in the city centre, Central Business District organizations struggled to move on. Pressures mounted, impacting the leadership and culture within these organizations, stretching their networks of relationships, and reducing their ability to absorb additional change. Their resilience suffered because of it, and these organizations in particular became even more vulnerable to future events.

As the Christchurch earthquakes illustrated, resilience is not static – it ebbs and flows like a tide. For your organization, it may not be a series of

Figure 1.3 Resilience for organizations across all sectors collapses following the 22 February 2011 earthquake

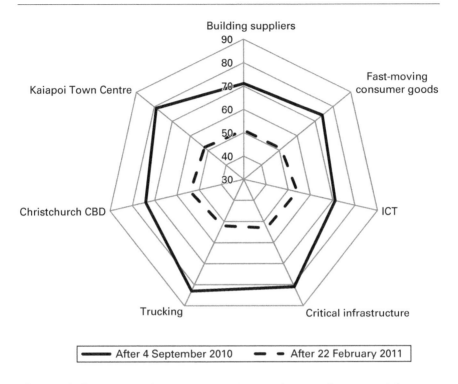

Figure 1.4 Resilience for organizations in most, but not all, sectors of the Canterbury economy rebuilds, 15 months after the 22 February 2011 earthquake

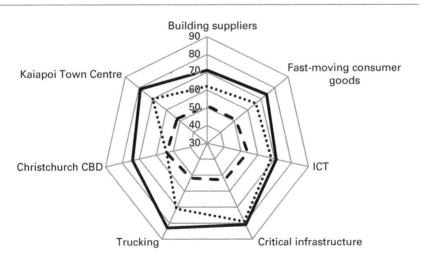

earthquakes that erodes your resilience – it could be ongoing pressures to reduce costs, subtle shifts in customer behaviour, a souring internal culture or frequent restructuring; any of these and many other things can knock the resilience out of your organization.

Since resilience is dynamic, it is important to monitor how your organization's resilience evolves over time. Once you can see how normal business changes are affecting resilience, you can then become more intentional about the way you manage and grow resilience.

Managing resilience as a strategic asset

Walmart was the darling of the response to Hurricane Katrina.[13] Before Katrina struck, it would be fair to say that Walmart had an embattled public reputation. It faced regular controversies over its treatment of employees, for selling goods made in foreign sweatshops, the impact it was having on smaller local retailers, and just about every other aspect of its operations. In April 2005, just four months before Katrina struck, *Fortune* magazine described Walmart as marching 'itself straight into a management and public relations quagmire'.[14] Walmart, however, managed to become the hero of the response to Hurricane Katrina, donating heavily towards relief campaigns, opening its stores and giving away supplies to affected residents. It partnered with the Red Cross to deliver relief supplies within days, into areas that the government couldn't reach for several weeks.

'A lot of you are going to have to make decisions above your level. Make the best decision that you can with the information that's available to you at the time, and, above all, do the right thing.'[15] This was the message CEO Lee Scott delivered to store managers as Katrina approached. It set the tone for the response that was to follow. At a corporate level, Walmart proactively used its own hurricane-tracking software to understand where the storm was likely to make landfall. It then filled trucks with supplies that would be needed by devastated communities, and staged them just outside the expected landfall zone. As soon as the hurricane passed, these trucks were ready to be deployed. Being proactive and leveraging its world-class logistics capabilities, Walmart not only managed to deliver relief for those directly affected by the storm, but also to deliver the organization a much-needed public relations boost.

Just before he stepped down, Leslie Dach (Executive Vice President of Corporate Affairs at Walmart) described how Hurricane Katrina became a watershed moment for the company: 'For Walmart, the turning point was Hurricane

Katrina. When the storm hit, we mobilized to provide meals, emergency supplies, and cash. No internal debate was needed—those were obvious right things to do. But the experience opened our eyes to the broader opportunity to make a difference.'

Two months later, then-CEO Lee Scott gave a landmark speech in which he asked: 'What would it take for Walmart to be at our best all the time? What if we used our size and resources to make this country and this earth an even better place for all of us? And what if we could do that and build a stronger business at the same time?'[16]

Remember Deborah Pretty's study from earlier, looking at the frequency of crises for the world't largest 1,000 organizations? Deborah came across another surprising discovery, finding that organizations that managed their crisis well actually came out of it with a share price higher than it was before. Looking at what happened to share market values following each crisis, she identified clear patterns between recoverers and non-recoverers. Figure 1.5 shows average adjusted share market values for the year after the crisis (stripping out the effect of market influences and other factors unrelated to the crisis) for each group.

Figure 1.5   The effect of crises on share market value – the differing pathways of recoverers vs non-recoverers (adapted from Knight and Pretty, 2001)[17]

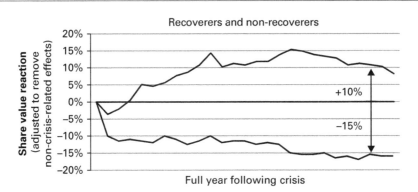

Crises present an opportunity for the stock market and analysts to gain insight into an organization's management capability to deal with the unexpected and extreme. Figure 1.5 shows that the market makes its judgement on this capability rapidly. Within just the first few days of a crisis emerging, organizations are quickly differentiated into those on a trajectory of recovery and those that are not, highlighting the importance of being ready to respond effectively.

Deborah's study also demonstrates that crises don't have to be all about managing the downside. Crises can be transformational, and more resilient organizations can turn their crises into opportunities to become better than before. Organizations that managed their crises well were able to outperform the market by around 10 per cent – in other words, they gained value as a consequence. Crises create windows of opportunity for change – be it technology change, developing new partnerships and collaborations, reassessing your organization's business proposition or renewing commitment to your organization's core values. These windows of opportunity are often fleeting, and you need to be both open and positioned to take advantage of them.

Reaping the benefits today

While it is easy to demonstrate the benefits of resilience for organizations that experience a crisis, one of the most exciting findings from the latest research is that the value from resilience doesn't *just* emerge during times of crisis. There are tangible business-as-usual benefits from having a more resilient organization. Evidence is starting to emerge that resilient organizations are also more likely to have better cash flow and to be more profitable.

Back in 2010, one of our PhD students, Amy Stephenson, undertook a study of 61 organizations in Auckland, New Zealand's largest city, to compare and contrast their resilience strengths and weaknesses.[18] What she discovered were statistically significant relationships showing that organizations with higher resilience were also more likely to have better cash flow, greater profitability and better return on investment.

The sample size in Amy's Auckland study wasn't particularly large, so in 2013 we looked to see if we could replicate the results in a different study – this time looking at how organizations were recovering from the Canterbury earthquakes. In the Canterbury study, we collected information on 541 organizations, randomly selected from across the region's economy.[19] This time, we found that not only had the more resilient organizations recovered better and faster from the earthquakes, but, once again, there were statistically significant correlations indicating that more resilient organizations were also more likely to have better cash flow and to be more profitable (Table 1.1).

Categorizing our sample into two groups – organizations with below- and above-average resilience – we compared their responses to questions on

Table 1.1 Comparisons of cash flow and profitability status of organizations with above- and below-average resilience

		Organizations with below-average resilience (%)	Organizations with above-average resilience (%)
Cash flow	Poor or very poor	14	7
	Satisfactory	35	27
	Good or excellent	51	65
Profit	Unprofitable or breaking even	29	18
	Moderately profitable	61	64
	Highly profitable	10.5	18

cash flow and profitability. Organizations with below-average resilience were more likely also to have poor or very poor cash flow. Fourteen per cent of such organizations had poor or very poor cash flow – compared to only 7 per cent of organizations with above-average resilience. Organizations with below-average resilience were also more likely to be unprofitable or just breaking even. Twenty-nine per cent of such organizations were unprofitable or just breaking even – compared to 18 per cent of organizations with above-average resilience.

Looking at the other end of the spectrum, organizations with above-average resilience had a higher likelihood of having good or excellent cash flow (65 per cent), compared to organizations with below-average resilience (51 per cent). They were also more likely to be highly profitable compared to their less resilient counterparts – with the proportion of high profitability increasing from 10.5 up to 18 per cent.

A key question for us, as researchers, is: which is the cause and which is the effect? Is it that resilience-enhancing behaviours within organizations are also leading to better business-as-usual performance? Or is it that once an organization has its business-as-usual activities performing well, it has the resources and capacity to invest more in its resilience? At present, we don't have the data to untangle the directionality of these relationships, but we are now embarking on a project that may give us some of the answers. We are going back to our Christchurch organizations, five years and several earthquakes later, to see how both their business performance and their resilience are tracking. Using these longitudinal datasets, comparing then vs now, we hope to be able to see the extent to which resilience drives business performance and vice versa, and the particular characteristics of organizations that have the capacity to drive both.

When you look at the indicators of an organization's resilience (which we will come to shortly), it starts to become clear why there is a relationship between resilience and business performance. Many of the qualities that support resilience in an organization – good leadership and culture, strong networks and relationships, and being change-ready – also offer tangible benefits to the way an organization operates in the day-to-day.

Resilient organizations understand the need to be able to change and adapt quickly, not just to crises but to any form of change happening in their world. They therefore foster innovation and creativity within their teams and encourage information and ideas to flow across the organization. They work hard to ensure that they have highly engaged and networked staff, and foster an environment of high trust. They invest in leadership throughout the organization and channel people's efforts towards a clear purpose. They actively develop partnerships and networks that they can both leverage in the day-to-day and call on when they need to. All of these features will sound very familiar to anyone striving to create high-performing organizations in business-as-usual environments!

While the research on the link between resilience and day-to-day business performance is still in its early stages, the potential of these findings is tantalizing. Resilience offers the opportunity to take on more risk and to out-compete other organizations to capture the opportunities that come with change. To achieve the full benefits of resilience, however, organizations need to practise resilience every day. They need to integrate it fully into business-as-usual practices. As my colleague John Vargo often says, 'you don't get good at something unless you practise'.

When people hear the fire alarm go off in their building, they don't stop to read the evacuation instructions before heading for the exits. They respond intuitively to the situation. Making the correct response feel 'intuitive' is developed through years of fire drills until it becomes embedded as our natural response. Organizations need to apply the same principles for ingraining resilience thinking and behaviours into their organization's DNA.

The drive for organizations to become more resilient is not just a selfish one to achieve profitability and longevity for the organization. There are significant community benefits to be gained when organizations within our communities become more resilient. Organizations are like a keystone species within our communities – they touch nearly every part of our lives.

Organizations own, manage and maintain our critical infrastructure. They provide goods and services that residents want and need. They enable our economy to function, and provide both employment and gathering places that bring people together. If we can make our organizations more resilient, they become better employers, they provide better goods and services to their customers, and they provide stability for communities during turbulent times. Creating more resilient organizations is an important step towards creating more resilient communities.

The ingredients of resilience

Over 10 years, our research programme Resilient Organisations has grown to involve more than 35 active researchers, bringing together people with diverse expertise, perspectives and ways of framing the organizational resilience challenge. Together, our team has identified 13 indicators to look for, to identify how resilient an organization is (Figure 1.6).

Figure 1.6 Indicators of organizational resilience

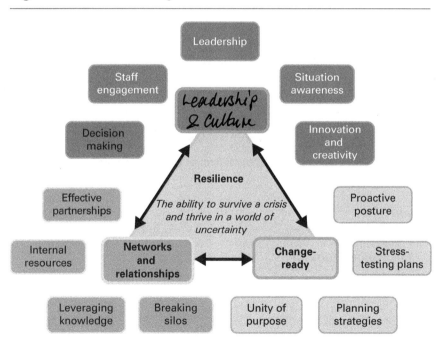

No matter what the type of organization, large or small, for-profit or not-for-profit, the same 13 indicators of resilience apply. Within these 13 indicators, however, our team believes that some indicators are more potent than others. In this book I will take you through the top five ingredients for creating a resilient organization:

- Ingredient 1: Leaders people want to follow (leadership)
- Ingredient 2: Having a team of engaged people (staff engagement)
- Ingredient 3: Having 3am friends (effective partnerships)
- Ingredient 4: Keeping a finger on the pulse (situation awareness)
- Ingredient 5: Moving to a mindset of constantly learning (innovation and creativity).

Resilience is a capability that must be proactively fostered and maintained over time. Over the next chapters I will give you ideas of tangible things that that you can do within your organization to actively improve its resilience – starting today!

Through our research we have helped develop a number of tools for evaluating an organization's current level of resilience. On the following page are a series of 13 questions which we use in our research to profile an organization rapidly. We call this tool the Resilience Thumbprint.[20] This tool provides a snapshot of your organization's current resilience strengths and weaknesses, which will help you to identify the particular sections of this book that are most important for you to focus on.

At the end of this chapter and in the resilience initiatives section, there is more information on ways to actually benchmark and evaluate your organization's resilience and to track it over time.[21]

Quick Start Guide: Evaluate your own organization's resilience

Table 1.2 Resilience Thumbprint questions for identifying resilience strengths and weaknesses

Resilience Thumbprint

To what extent do you agree or disagree with the following statements for your organization?

*Score your organization against each of the indicators on a scale of 0 to 10

   10 = completely agree; this is an area of strength for our organization.

   0 = completely disagree; this is an area of significant weakness for our organization.

Resilience indicator	Statement	Score (0–10)*
Leadership (pages 31–45)	There would be good leadership from within our organization if we were struck by a crisis.	
Staff engagement (pages 51–68)	People in our organization are committed to working on a problem until it is resolved.	
Effective partnerships (pages 76–82)	We build relationships with others we might have to work with in a crisis.	
Situation awareness (pages 93–108)	We proactively monitor our industry to have an early warning of emerging issues.	
Innovation and creativity (pages 111–125)	We are known for our ability to use knowledge in novel ways.	
Proactive posture (pages 141–142)	We have a focus on being able to respond to the unexpected.	
Unity of purpose (pages 142–143)	We have clearly defined priorities for what is important during and after a crisis.	
Decision making (page 137)	We can make tough decisions quickly.	
Breaking silos (pages 143–144)	There are few barriers stopping us from working well with other organizations.	
Internal resources (pages 37–39)	Our organization maintains sufficient resources to absorb some unexpected change.	
Leveraging knowledge (pages 140–141)	If key people were unavailable, there are always others who could fill their role.	

(Continued)

Table 1.2 (Continued)

Resilience indicator	Statement	Score (0–10)*
Planning strategies (pages 132–133)	Given how others depend on us, the way we plan for the unexpected is appropriate.	☐
Stress-testing plans (page 135)	Our organization is committed to practising and testing its emergency plans to ensure they are effective.	☐

By looking at how you scored your organization, you can now see your organization's broad areas of strengths and weaknesses from a resilience perspective. You are probably guessing that I'm now going to suggest you select your areas of greatest weakness and work on those first. But I'm not. Instead I'm going to suggest that you identify your organization's areas of strength and to use these to build your resilience further.

Why? Because managers often see themselves as problem solvers whose job is to 'fix what's broken' in the organization. But there is much to be gained from focusing on what is working well, and building on that success. It turns out that we learn better and are able to improve task performance when we focus on our successes rather than our failures.

In the 1980s, sports psychologist Daniel Kirschenbaum ran an experiment to understand the effect of positive and negative reinforcement on how people learn a new skill such as bowling.[22] He took a group of beginner bowlers and gave them all the same lesson on good bowling technique before the start of a five-week league competition. One group of bowlers was asked to review their performance after each bowling session, focusing on what they did well. Before their next time bowling, this group was prompted to remember those things they had done well in the previous session.

The second group of bowlers was asked to review their performance after each session and identify what they had done poorly. This group was prompted to remind themselves of these problems before their next session, to avoid making the same mistakes in the following rounds.

Which group of bowlers do you think improved their bowling performance? The bowlers who focused on what they did well showed a much greater improvement in bowling scores when compared with the other group.

We all have our areas of natural strength and weakness. The same is true for any organization. There will be things that come naturally within your organization because of its history, the sector in which it operates and the type of people it employs. Focusing on strengthening areas of natural talent can provide great rewards and can be less daunting to take on as an initial step, compared with tackling an entrenched area of weakness.

Donald Clifton and James Harter from the Gallup Organization give a great example of how this concept can apply in the business world.[23] They worked with a major brewery that managed more than 7,000 pubs across England. When a pub's performance started to drop, the management response was usually to redecorate. As a result, there was generally an improvement in the pub's result, but it didn't last. Before long, the pub would be back to being one of the company's poorest performers. The researchers asked why the company was spending its entire refurbishment budget on the lowest-performing pubs. Shouldn't the top-performing pubs also get refurbished when they get a bit worn?

The brewery decided to experiment. It refurbished eight of its top-performing pubs and eight of its low-performing pubs to see which would be the better investment. It soon discovered that putting money into making its top-performing pubs even better was by far the better investment. The eight high-performing pubs had the greatest percentage increases in profitability, even when the percentages were computed on a much larger base. For the same amount of cost and effort, the refurbished high-volume pubs were seven times more profitable than the average refurbished low-volume pub. Why? After looking at differences in location, local competition and other factors, it became clear that the distinguishing feature of the high-volume pubs was the calibre of the individuals working within them. Refurbishing the high-volume pubs was basically placing the investment in an area of natural strength for the organization – in the hands of its best people.

The idea that it is easier to improve on an area of strength rather than an area of weakness has been around for a long time. In the 1950s, there was a large state-wide research study undertaken in Nebraska to evaluate the effectiveness of different teaching methods.[24] About 6,000 tenth-graders participated in the study. While analysing the data, the researchers observed an interesting result. While all children improved their reading skills in the course of the study, those children who already had better reading skills at the start of the research were the ones who achieved the most gains. This was an unexpected result. It became the seed for a hypothesis – that individuals gain more when they build on their talents than when they make comparable efforts to improve their areas of weakness.

We can't always just focus on the positives, though – weaknesses do need to be addressed. My advice is to tackle both your areas of greatest strength and your areas of greatest weakness *together*. Leverage areas of existing strength to help address weaknesses. For example, if your organization is strong on building effective partnerships with other organizations but weak on stress-testing plans, invite some of your partner organizations who *are* good at stress-testing plans to coach your organization. If your organization is strong on planning strategies but weak on staff engagement, utilize your planning capabilities to design and implement a forward work programme to improve staff engagement. If your organization is strong on innovation and creativity but weak on traditional planning strategies, use that innovation and creativity to discover new and different ways of planning that might work better for your organization.

Summary

Here are some key take-outs from this chapter:

- Resilient organizations are future-ready – with an inbuilt capacity not only to weather the storms of change, but able to thrive in such environments.

- Research has identified 13 indicators of organizational resilience. Leadership, staff engagement, effective partnerships, situation awareness, and innovation and creativity are particularly potent.

- As your organization goes through normal changes, its level of resilience will fluctuate. It is important, therefore, to monitor your organization's resilience and put in strategies to maintain and grow resilience over time.

- Resilience has business-as-usual benefits. More resilient organizations are more likely to have good cash flow and to be profitable. There are also significant community benefits to be gained when the organizations within our communities become more resilient.

- Crises are not rare and unusual. Every organization is likely to face at least one disruptive crisis during its life. But it is not all bad – crises come hand in hand with opportunities if your organization is ready to capture them.

- No matter what size, sector or type of organization you are with, the ideas in this book will help you to make your organization more resilient.

Resilience initiatives – monitoring resilience over time

At the end of this book are a number of different initiatives for improving resilience. The ones most relevant to getting the resilience conversation started within your organization, and for measuring and monitoring resilience over time, are:

1 Get someone in to tell their story.

2 Take advantage of burning platforms.

3 Use a little peer pressure.

4 Let it be their idea.

5 Don't call it Resilience.

6 Use the Resilience HealthCheck to generate discussion and reflection.

7 Test the waters using the Resilience Thumbprint.

8 Benchmark the resilience of your organization.

9 Partner with other organizations to benchmark and improve resilience together.

10 Audit resilience capabilities.

References and further reading

If you are not based within a research organization, copies of academic papers can sometimes be difficult or expensive to source. I suggest searching the paper title on Google Scholar: https://scholar.google.com Once you find the paper you are after, click on the link that takes you to all versions of the paper. Often pre-publication copies of papers are archived within publicly accessible research repositories or on authors' personal websites. The internet changes over time. The web-links provided throughout this book are current as at July 2016.

1 Swiss Air collapse:
   - Gow, D (2007) Executives on trial over Swissair collapse, *The Guardian*, 17 January
   - Hermann, A and Rammal, HG (2010) The grounding of the 'flying bank', *Management Decision*, **48**, pp 1048–62
   - Rues, R (2005) *What Role Does Organisational Culture Play in Organisational Resilience: A case study of SAir Group (Swissair) 1998–2001.*

Originally published in German: Rues, R (2005) Bruchlandung–Krisen-Widerstandsfähigkeit der Swissair, *RISKNEWS*, **2** (5), pp 50–54. English translation published by MinimaRisk, http://www.minimarisk.com/swissair-risk-management/

– Sims, RR and Sauser, WI (2013) Toward a better understanding of the relationships among received wisdom, groupthink, and organizational ethical culture, *Journal of Management Policy and Practice*, **14** (4), pp 75–90

– The Economist (2001) A scary Swiss meltdown: how a dud strategy brought a solid company to the brink of bankruptcy, *The Economist*, 19 July

– The Economist (2001) Uncharted airspace, *The Economist*, 20 September

– Knorr, A and Arndt, A (2003) *Swissair's collapse – an economic analysis.* Inst. für Weltwirtschaft und Internationales Management

2 Rues, R (2005) *What Role Does Organisational Culture Play in Organisational Resilience: A case study of SAir Group (Swissair) 1998–2001.* Originally published in German: Rues, R (2005) Bruchlandung–Krisen-Widerstandsfähigkeit der Swissair, *RISKNEWS*, **2** (5), pp 50–54. English translation published by MinimaRisk, http://www.minimarisk.com/swissair-risk-management/

3 Resilient Organisations is a New Zealand social enterprise that carries out public-good science research with global reach. We are a multidisciplinary team of over 35 researchers, representing a synthesis of engineering, science and business leadership aimed at transforming organizations so that they can successfully survive major disruptions, avoid chronic dysfunction, build robust partnerships, and prosper. You can find out more about our work, and download free resources for your organization, at www.resorgs.org.nz

4 Deborah Pretty and Rory Knight have undertaken a number of studies looking at the effect of crises on shareholder value. The statistics discussed in this chapter can be found in Pretty (2002), but other papers of theirs are also worth reading:

– Pretty, D (2002) *Risks That Matter: Sudden increases and decreases in shareholder value and the implications for CEOs*, Oxford Metrica, http://www.oxfordmetrica.com/public/cms/files/599/02repcomey.pdf

– Knight, RF and Pretty, DJ (2001) *Reputation & Value: The case of corporate catastrophes*, Oxford Metrica, http://www.oxfordmetrica.com/public/CMS/Files/488/01RepComAIG.pdf

– Knight, RF and Pretty, DJ (1999) Corporate catastrophes, stock returns, and trading volume,*Corporate Reputation Review*, **2** (4), pp 363–78

– Knight, RF and Pretty, DJ (1998) Value at risk: the effects of catastrophes on share price, *Risk Management*, **45** (5), pp 39–41

5 Stephenson, A (2011) *Benchmarking the Resilience of Organisations*, University of Canterbury, PhD thesis, http://www.resorgs.org.nz/images/stories/pdfs/thesis_benchmarking%20the%20resilience%20of%20organisations.pdf

6 Nokia and Ericsson:

– Mukherjee, AS (2008) The fire that changed an industry: a case study on thriving in a networked world, *The Financial Times*, 1 October, http://www.ftpress.com/articles/article.aspx?p=1244469

– Berggren, C and Bengtsson, L (2004) Rethinking outsourcing in manufacturing: a tale of two telecom firms, *European Management Journal*, **22** (2), pp 211–23

– Latour, A (2001) A fire in Albuquerque sparks crisis for European cell-phone giants: Nokia handles shock with aplomb as Ericsson of Sweden gets burned, *The Wall Street Journal*, 29 January, http://www.wsj.com/articles/SB980720939804883010

– Sheffi, Y and Rice Jr, JB (2005) A supply chain view of the resilient enterprise, *MIT Sloan Management Review*, **47** (1), pp 41–48

7 Ericsson (2000) Ericsson Annual Report 2000, http://www.ericsson.com/res/investors/docs/annual-reports-1970-2002/annual2000_understanding_en.pdf

8 Mukherjee, AS (2008) The fire that changed an industry: a case study on thriving in a networked world, *The Financial Times*, 1 October, http://www.ftpress.com/articles/article.aspx?p=1244469

9 Sheffi, Y (2005) *The Resilient Enterprise*, The MIT Press, Cambridge, MA

10 For details of that initial research see:

– McManus, S, Seville, E, Vargo, J *et al* (2008) facilitated process for improving organizational resilience, *Natural Hazards Review*, **9** (1), pp 81–90

– McManus, S, Seville, E, Vargo, J *et al* (2007) *Resilience Management: A framework for assessing and improving the resilience of organisations*, Resilient Organisations Research Report 2007/01, http://www.resorgs.org.nz/images/stories/pdfs/resilience%20management%20research%20report%20resorgs%2007-01.pdf

11 Lapowsky, I (2014) Livestrong without Lance, *Inc. Magazine*, **4**, http://www.inc.com/magazine/201404/issie-lapowsky/what-livestrong-is-like-without-lance-armstrong.html

12 Sugrue, TJ (2014) *The Origins of the Urban Crisis: Race and inequality in postwar Detroit*, Princeton University Press, Princeton, PA

13 Walmart and Hurricane Katrina:

– Mattera, P (2005) Disaster as relief: how Wal-Mart used Hurricane Katrina to repair its image, *Corporate Research*, E-Letter No 55, September–October

– Horwitz, S (2008) Making hurricane response more effective: lessons from the private sector and the coast guard during Katrina, *Mercatus Policy Comment*, 17, http://dx.doi.org/10.2139/ssrn.1350554

– Colten, CE, Kates, RW and Laska, SB (2008) *Community Resilience: Lessons from New Orleans and Hurricane Katrina*, Community and Regional

Resilience Initiative (CARRI), Report **3**, Oak Ridge National Laboratory, http://www.resilientus.org/wp-content/uploads/2013/03/FINAL_COLTEN_9-25-08_1223482263.pdf

14 Serwer, A (2005) Bruised in Bentonville, *FORTUNE Magazine*, 18 April, http://archive.fortune.com/magazines/fortune/fortune_archive/2005/04/18/8257005/index.htm

15 Horwitz, S (2009) Wal-Mart to the rescue: private enterprise's response to Hurricane Katrina, *The Independent Review*, **13** (4), pp 511–28

16 Dach, L (2013) Don't spin a better story. Be a better company, *Harvard Business Review*, October

17 Knight, RF and Pretty, DJ (2001) *Reputation & Value: The case of corporate catastrophes*, Oxford Metrica, http://www.oxfordmetrica.com/public/CMS/Files/488/01RepComAIG.pdf

18 For details on Amy's research see:

– Stephenson, A, Seville, E, Vargo, J *et al* (2010) *Benchmark Resilience: A study of the resilience of organisations in the Auckland region*, Resilient Organisations Research Report 2010/03b, http://www.resorgs.org.nz/images/stories/pdfs/benchmark%20resilience%20-%20resorgs%20research%20reportb.pdf

– Lee, A, Seville, E and Vargo, J (2013) Developing a tool to measure and compare organizations, *Natural Hazards Review*, **14** (1), pp 29–41

19 Economics of Resilient Infrastructure project:

– Project website: http://www.resorgs.org.nz/Our-Research/economics-of-resilient-infrastructure.html

– Brown, C, Stevenson, J, Giovinazzi, S *et al* (2015) Factors influencing impacts on and recovery trends of organisations: evidence from the 2010/2011 Canterbury earthquakes, *International Journal of Disaster Risk Reduction*, **14** (1), pp 56–72

– Seville, E, Stevenson, J, Brown, C *et al* (2014) *Disruption and Resilience: How organisations coped with the Canterbury earthquakes*, ERI Research Report 2014/002, http://www.resorgs.org.nz/images/stories/pdfs/Organisationsfacingcrisis/disruption_and_resilience.pdf

20 Resilience Thumbprint Tool:

– For more details and to access the tool online for free, see: http://www.resorgs.org.nz/Resources/resilience-thumbprint-tool.html

– Whitman, ZR, Kachali, H, Roger, D *et al* (2013) Short-form version of the Benchmark Resilience Tool (BRT-53), *Measuring Business Excellence*, **17** (3), pp 3–14

21 There are several tools available for evaluating resilience; in particular, see:

– Resilience Benchmark Tool: http://www.resorgs.org.nz/benchmark-resilience-tool.html

- Resilience HealthCheck Tool: http://www.organisationalresilience.gov.au/HealthCheck/Pages/default.aspx
- Resilience Thumbprint Tool: http://www.resorgs.org.nz/Resources/resilience-thumbprint-tool.html
- Employee Resilience Tool: http://www.resorgs.org.nz/Resources/employee-resilience-tool.html

22 Kirschenbaum, DS, Ordman, AM, Tomarken, AJ *et al* (1982) Effects of differential self-monitoring and level of mastery on sports performance: brain power bowling, *Cognitive Therapy and Research*, **6** (3), pp 335–41

23 Clifton, DO and Harter, JK (2003) Investing in strengths, in *Positive Organizational Scholarship: Foundations of a new discipline*, ed AKS Cameron, BJE Dutton and CRE Quinn, Berrett-Koehler, San Francisco

24 Glock, JW (1955) *The Relative Value of Three Methods of Improving Reading: Tachistocscope, films and determined effort*, PhD Thesis, University of Nebraska–Lincoln. Referenced in Clifton, DO and Harter, JK (2003) Investing in strengths, in *Positive Organizational Scholarship: Foundations of a new discipline*, ed AKS Cameron, BJE Dutton and CRE Quinn, Berrett-Koehler, San Francisco

Leadership – leaders people want to follow

02

As the final whistle blew on the quarter-final of the 2007 Rugby World Cup, the All Blacks, one of the best and most consistent sporting teams in the world, had failed once again in their bid to become World Champions.

The All Blacks, New Zealand's national rugby team, have an unrivalled track record.[1] In their 109-year history, the All Blacks have won 75 per cent of their international test matches. This is a remarkable statistic. Brazil's five-time world champion football team has a success rate in international matches of just 62 per cent.

But for all their success, winning the Rugby World Cup had eluded the All Blacks for the past 20 years. After winning the inaugural Rugby World Cup tournament in 1987, they had since suffered numerous defeats. The 2007 Rugby World Cup tournament was the All Black's opportunity to rectify a 20-year World Cup drought.

They were leading favourites for the tournament, having won nearly every trophy going over the preceding two years. They cruised through the pool games into the quarter-finals. Everyone was expecting their game against France to be an easy win.

After leading the French 13–3 at half time, all was going to plan. But by the end of the game, the All Blacks had crashed and burnt out of the tournament, losing 18–20. The team was devastated and the hopes of a nation left in tatters.

The fallout was immediate. There were calls across the New Zealand media for the coaching team to be sacked. History didn't bode well for Graham Henry, the lead coach. Following each previous World Cup failure, the incumbent coaches had retired, resigned or were unceremoniously dumped by the New Zealand Rugby Union.

In the face of intense public scrutiny and debate, somehow Graham managed to convince the Rugby Union that he had unfinished business. He was given four more years as coach to try to win the World Cup in 2011.

How do you take players devastated by failure and turn them back into a winning team? Graham set about fostering a culture of shared and collective leadership, where followers become leaders and leaders knew when to follow. The players and the coaching and management staff became equal partners in working towards a shared vision of success.

Graham identified a cohort of seven senior players, each with exceptional leadership skills. These players later became known as the Magnificent Seven. Four of the seven players were to be on-field leaders, becoming heavily involved in reviewing performance and developing game plan strategies. The other three were to be off-field leaders, responsible for the culture and morale within the team, setting boundaries around acceptable off-field behaviours and integrating new members into the team culture.

Four years later, in 2011, the All Blacks again faced their nemesis, France – this time in the Rugby World Cup final. In a heart-stopping 80 minutes, where every point was hard fought, this time the All Blacks managed to hold their nerve and come out the victors 8–7.

So what made this time different? In nearly all the preceding World Cup tournaments, the All Blacks had been the team with the best form, but they had never been able to secure the win. Graham puts much of it down to the shared leadership model they implemented.

Leadership is not about a single person taking charge and providing the direction. No single person can ever hold all the qualities required to lead all people all the time. A head coach has a big influence on the team, but once the game starts, the players are on their own. They have to come together to make it happen. Leadership has to happen on the field.

Off the field, a teammate's peers are far more likely to influence the culture and acceptable norms of their team mates. Having to face up to the whole team and admit mistakes when boundaries are crossed, such as a late night out drinking, is far more difficult for a young man than being told off by a grumpy coach.

By leveraging the leadership skills within the team, the All Blacks had tapped into something far more potent than just a great coach and great players. They had a team that felt ownership. They had become a force to be reckoned with.

Four years later, in 2015, the All Blacks went on to win the World Cup again. They are the first team to win consecutive World Cups in the tournament's history, cementing their reputation as one of the world's top sports teams.

If it can happen for a sports team, then it can also happen for any organization. When faced with a major crisis, it is like a World Cup Final for your organization. Whether your organization rises to the challenge or flounders will be determined by the leadership and culture you have instilled in your organization over recent years.

Leadership is one of the most critical requirements for a resilient organization, and it is not just leadership at the top of the organization that matters. Whether you are the CEO of a major corporation, the owner of a small business, a middle manager or someone working at the front line of your organization's operation, the way that *you* demonstrate leadership every day has an influence on your organization's resilience.

An organization with exceptional leadership can get through just about any crisis, even with minimal preparation. The converse, however, is not true. Even with the best planning in the world, an organization with poor leadership is likely to stumble and fall at the first sign of real crisis.

So what sort of leadership is needed to build resilience? As shown in Figure 2.1, there are five key criteria: being true to your values, painting a vision of what is possible, having a visible presence, inspiring good leadership from others, and providing the right leadership for the time.

Figure 2.1 Be a leader people want to follow

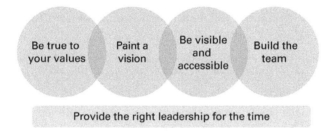

It sounds obvious, but leaders are nothing if people are not willing to be led by them. To earn the respect, loyalty and confidence of people that you lead there are several prerequisites, but the first requirement is establishing a connection with people on an emotional level.

Be true to your values

It would be fair to say that the government response to Hurricane Katrina in 2005 did not get off to a good start. Ten days after the hurricane made landfall, retired US Coast Guard Admiral Thad Allen was put in charge of turning around the response.[2] He started by calling together a meeting of the nearly 2,000 people he was leading.

Standing on a table with a bull horn, he gave everyone one order – to treat anybody they came into contact with that had been affected by the storm as if they were a member of their own family. They were to treat people how they would like *their* family to be treated in the same situation. If they did this, then any mistake made would be to err on the side of doing too much – and that was OK. Thad went on to say that if they did this and anyone has a problem with it, then the problem lies with the admiral and not those working on the front line.

And with that, a cheer broke out. Thad describes how there had been so much stress and pressure exerted on the response from the perception that it wasn't going well, that a simple set of core values – a North Star to steer by – was what people needed.

Thad Allen is widely recognized as an exceptional crisis leader, being credited with the turnaround in the federal response to Hurricane Katrina, managing New York harbour during 9/11, and being appointed National Incident Controller for the Deepwater Horizon oil spill. Thad believes a leader's key role is to secure unity of effort. The best way to achieve that unity of effort is to instil a set of shared values to which everyone involved can subscribe.

If you are like me, you will still remember the comment from Tony Haywood, CEO of BP at the time of the Deepwater Horizon oil spill. 'I want my life back' was the sound-bite that quickly became associated in many people's minds with BP's response. It was just five words out of many thousands that had been spoken about the crisis and the response, and yet it is these five words that are remembered – they made people feel that Haywood and BP simply didn't care.

When it comes to a crisis, it is matters of the heart on which you will be judged. Many years after the crisis has passed, the things that people will still remember are the issues that affected them emotionally. If your organization does not act responsibly or treat people fairly, this stigma will be carried for far longer than the direct impact of any crisis. This means that as a leader it is just as important to focus on '*doing what is right*' as on '*getting it right*'.

While every crisis is different, people are always involved. Reflecting on how your organization treats people, including staff, customers and the community in general, is therefore a good place to start in terms of thinking about whether your organization is managing matters of the heart effectively.

In 1982, seven people died in Chicago after taking extra strength Tylenol capsules which had been laced with cyanide.[3] Not waiting to see if the contamination was more widespread, Johnson and Johnson, the maker of Tylenol, immediately recalled all product in the Chicago area, finding three other bottles of cyanide-laced product that had not yet been consumed. The company then worked closely with authorities to identify the source of the contamination. It turned out to be a case of product tampering. With copycat acts starting to appear in other parts of the country, the company quickly issued a recall of all extra strength Tylenol capsules across the entire United States.

Johnson and Johnson's management of Tylenol tampering is one of the most commonly cited examples of excellent crisis management. It is a crisis that was well managed and therefore built long-term reputation for the organization.

'We believe our first responsibility is to the doctors, nurses and patients, to the mothers and fathers and all others who use our products and services'.[4] Written in 1940, this is the first line of Johnson and Johnson's Credo. While in today's world a product recall seems like an obvious response, back in 1982 product recalls were rarely used, let alone a recall of such scale. This recall involved not just one or two batches of product, but a whole product line involving 31 million bottles.

Although Johnson and Johnson was not responsible for the tampering, it made it very clear that it did not shirk away from its responsibility to ensure public safety. By demonstrating its commitment to 'people first, property second', the company pulled off something very special – it earned the trust and loyalty of its customers, which continues to this day.

What is surprising about Johnson and Johnson's experience is that so many organizations have failed to learn from it. Seven years later, when the oil tanker *Exxon Valdez* grounded in Alaska's Prince William Sound, spilling more than 11 million gallons of crude oil,[5] it took six days before the chairman of Exxon gave a statement to the media. He didn't go to Alaska until three long weeks after the crisis started. The effect? Exxon's leadership gave the distinct impression that damage to the environment was not important enough of an issue to involve its most senior leaders. This made any subsequent apologies issued by the company ring hollow for many, causing long-term loss of trust and reputation.

Over the years, there have been many more cases of organizations affronting the trust and core values of customers. In late 1999/early 2000, Ford and Firestone took months to adequately address issues associated with the tyres fitted to Ford Explorers.[6] The tyres were blowing out, with the tread separating while cars were driving at speed, leading to a number of fatal accidents. Perceptions of Ford and Firestone's initial response was that they were each trying to shift the blame to the other, when what the public really wanted to see was them working together to get the safety issue resolved quickly. A decade later, another car manufacturer, Toyota, was described by the assistant director of the FBI as putting 'sales over safety', and 'profit over principle', after covering up known safety issues with sticky pedals. Cars were accelerating out of control, leading to numerous deaths. Toyota eventually had to recall millions of vehicles and agreed to pay the US government $16.4m in fines over their slow response.[7]

A more recent case, yet again in the automobile industry, comes from Volkswagen, which was caught out fitting devices to diesel car models to falsely pass emissions test.[8] The devices could tell when the car was being tested in a laboratory – and when it was, the device would ramp up the pollution controls on the vehicle. Outside the laboratory environment, however, the device would reduce the emissions controls so that the car would deliver better performance. The company got away with this for many years, before being caught out. The apologies have been immediate, but also coupled with denials that those in the most senior positions knew about the fraudulent behaviour. The company will need to demonstrate some honest soul searching as to how its organizational culture allowed such behaviour to emerge, before many will accept that it is truly sorry for the behaviour, rather than just being sorry at being caught out.

Trust is one of those things that takes years to build up, but can be lost in an instant. A crisis is the time when trust is most needed, and yet is most fragile. It can be tempting to think that the situation is so extenuating that the normal principles by which you do business no longer apply. Unusual times do sometimes require unusual responses, but the core values of your organization should remain true. These core values underpin your organization – setting the tone, making it the place it is to work in, and permeating through to the way your organization deals with its customers. To throw core values out the window in a crisis very quickly erodes trust in both the organization and its leaders.

In 2012, an Australian researcher, Robert Kay, interviewed 50 CEOs of leading Australian companies in order to understand their perspectives on resilience. An interesting theme from that research was how CEOs identified trust as a central tenet of resilience: 'At its most simplistic, if you can't predict what other people will do under stress, then you can't trust them, which leads people to focus more on their own wellbeing, potentially at the expense of the organization and those around them'.[9]

In other words, a key feature of trust is having confidence in the way a situation will be approached. As a leader, it is not enough to 'do the right thing' when it is in your best interests to do so. Respect and confidence are earned when there is a consistent commitment to doing the right thing as a matter of principle.

Paint the vision

In 2005, Mississippi Power faced the challenge of reconnecting its entire customer base of 195,000 households, which had lost power during Hurricane Katrina.[10] When Mississippi Power engineers sat down to map out how they were going to do it, they came up with a plan that would see their customers reconnected within four weeks.

As the engineers presented their plan, Anthony Topazi, President of Mississippi Power, walked to the whiteboard and wrote '9-11-05'; 11 September. Topazi had just laid the challenge to take that terrible date and make it mean something positive. Mississippi Power made it its goal to get all homes reconnected by 11 September – just 12 days away.[11]

Four weeks to 12 days – it was a definite stretch-target. But, once the challenge was set, the Mississippi Power team knew what they were aiming for and, most importantly, they were supported to make it happen. If necessity is the mother of all invention, then, basically, what Topazi had done was to say: 'It's not going to work doing it the way that you normally do it. Come up with a new way of doing it.' They had to think outside the box.

The incredible part of this story is that they achieved it – every house that could receive power received it by nightfall on 10 September, one day early.

So how did they do it? Practically they achieved it by leveraging their usual workforce of 1,200 employees, to managing more than nine times that number of people helping with the repair effort (but more on that part of the story in the next chapter). From a leadership perspective, Mississippi Power achieved it through walking the talk of its corporate values, which are written on each and every employee's ID card – 'Unquestionable Trust, Superior Performance, and Total Commitment'.

Just a few decades ago, a hurricane response effort at Mississippi Power would have been run from the top down, with senior leaders directing what to do. Mississippi Power has turned this on its head to create a decentralized structure. Crews report to substations with a simple mission: Get the power on. People are trusted to do whatever it takes to deliver on the mission. Company procedures become less important than the ability to improvise. Everyone is empowered to engineer their own solutions – even out-of-state crews.

From this environment, creativity emerged. One crew chief stripped a generator off an ice machine to get a substation working. Others scavenged parts from fallen poles. Administration staff were making costly purchases instantly over the phone. And it worked. With a clear and simple mission, people got more done.

With no clear mission and no stretch-targets, there is often no sense of urgency or commitment. Putting a line in the sand, however, can feel like a very bold move. Once articulated, it is easy for critics to come back at you if the stretch-target is not achieved. While that's a risk, the greater risk is not putting any lines in the sand at all. Most of us have experienced working on a project with no deadlines. You can suddenly realize that a month, or a year, has passed and, while there has been progress, it isn't nearly as much as you were expecting. As a leader, you need to paint a vision for your team of what they can achieve, if they pull together.

Be visible and accessible

When he was mayor of New York City, Rudolf Giuliani[12] made it his personal policy to see with his own eyes the scene of every crisis. He wanted to evaluate the situation first-hand, believing there is only so much that somebody else can tell you about the crisis you are facing. People use their own lens to make sense of a situation imposing their own distortions. What one person describes as big, another might think is small. Giuliani felt it far better to see a situation with his own eyes and be able to make his own judgements.

Giuliani's need to be present potentially contributed to the fateful decision to locate New York's Emergency Command Center, 7 World Trade Center, close to the mayoral office. On 11 September, when the planes struck the World Trade Center towers, the Emergency Command Center became unusable. It was situated right beside the North Tower of the World Trade Center.

As the North Tower collapsed, it sent debris into 7 Trade Center, requiring immediate evacuation, igniting fires and causing the building's eventual collapse. The mayor now had to lead the biggest crisis response of his life – with none of the equipment, communications or systems on which his team would normally rely.

While locating the Emergency Command Center so close to a potential terrorist target was a dubious decision, it is the next decision that provides real insight into Giuliani's leadership style. Faced with the devastation of downtown New York, Giuliani had to decide where to go to set up an alternative command centre. The most immediate backup command post was nearby at the Police Department, but that had no electricity. The next functional backup command post was in Brooklyn, right across the Brooklyn Bridge. But Giuliani was reluctant to move out of Manhattan. He didn't want to be a bridge or tunnel away from the site. He instead chose to activate a virtual command centre in a nearby Police Precinct.

In his book *Leadership*,[13] Giuliani explains how being downtown – physically near the scene – was important. 'I wanted the fire commanders to talk to me face to face to look into my eyes and give me an undiluted assessment,' he wrote.

For anyone, it is difficult to make decisions about something you have never experienced before. To receive a written or verbal situation report, describing what is happening, is quite a different experience from seeing it with your own eyes.

When Giuliani first arrived downtown, he was told that people were throwing themselves from the World Trade Center. But the concept of people throwing themselves out of a building, 100 stories up, was too foreign for his mind to comprehend. Looking up, he saw debris coming off the buildings but no people. He dismissed the information as exaggeration.

It was only later, when Giuliani looked up again, and this time saw for himself someone climb out a window and jump, that the true enormity of what was occurring struck home. He went from feeling that he was dealing with a standard sort of emergency – the kind they plan for and could handle – to recognizing that it was much worse than anything they had ever faced before. He now understood that this was off the charts and they would need to come up with new ways to respond.

While we often view cynically the spectacle of political leaders flying in to visit disaster scenes, they do serve an important purpose. Receiving situation reports and updates only goes so far. A leader has to build his or her own understanding of the situation. Giuliani's visible presence was a defining feature of his leadership during the recovery from the 11 September World Trade Center attacks.

During a crisis, the pressures on a leader are many. It simply isn't possible to be everywhere and talk with everyone. It is important to think carefully, therefore, about whom you need to provide leadership to, and to make yourself visible and accessible for these people. A leader's reach needs to go beyond their direct reports; they also need to provide leadership to those at the front line of operations.

There are many circumstances where it may not be appropriate for you to actually be physically present, either because it is not safe or because it is more efficient for you to operate from elsewhere. In fact, often people working in emergency operation centres say that they find the presence of very senior leaders distracting and detrimental to the progress of the response. So, as a leader, how do you strike the balance between letting people get on with their job and you having a visible presence and demonstrating leadership within that situation?

My advice is to be intentional about making time to interact with people. At a formal level, this might take the form of providing regular briefings, but also look for informal opportunities to check in and see how people throughout your organization are coping. If there is a wind-down time at the end of a shift, take the time to drop in to catch up with people before they leave, to see how their day went. If there is a breakout or lunch room, take the opportunity to sit down once in a while to catch up – not to talk about work, but to get a sense of how they are doing.

As Thad Allen once put it, 'you need to lead from everywhere'. With a city in crisis and a complex recovery effort to coordinate, Rudolf Giuliani made the time to attend 200 funerals of those killed in the 9/11 attacks. Do not underestimate the importance of being present.

Build the team

Much of the discussion so far has focused on individuals providing leadership. But it is a myth that a good crisis leader is the one leading from the front, telling everyone what to do. One person cannot do it alone. Your organization doesn't just need a single charismatic leader; it needs a leadership team. But what if your organization's leaders don't seem interested in preparing for crises?

Unfortunately, research confirms what many of us suspect, that it can be very difficult to engage senior leaders in preparing for their crisis leadership role.[14] During the Cold War, few American presidents bothered to attend Pentagon exercises regularly.[15] More recently, in Switzerland, efforts to engage senior government leaders in crisis leadership exercises struck similar issues, with resistance coalescing around three key themes – no time, no need and no money. The reasons included: each crisis is unique, so it isn't possible to really prepare for them; standing operating procedures and checklists are useless; since crises come unexpectedly, it is better not to train and mistakenly think that one is ready; it is better to keep an open mind, to be adaptive and creative in a crisis; nowadays there is a constant and ongoing crisis so that everyday management equals crisis management, therefore no special training is required.[16]

In the late 2000s, the University of Canterbury in New Zealand was probably more prepared than many universities for crises.[17] It had emergency plans in place, and these were being exercised regularly by the operational team, but it would be fair to say that there was limited engagement with that planning by the senior management team.

So, in 2009, the university set about changing that by designing an Active Shooter exercise on campus, specifically to trigger the interest of the senior management team. The exercise scenario had two gunmen roaming the campus, taking shots at anyone they could see. There were already a number of known fatalities; the gunmen were still at large, last seen in the vicinity of the halls of residence. The university ran this exercise in conjunction with the Armed Offenders Squad (AOS) from the New Zealand Police. For the AOS, this was an opportunity for them to think through how they would hunt an armed offender in a complex building with many rooms, hallways and staircases, filled with innocents, many of whom fitted the profile of the offenders at large. The AOS had two of their own team members playing the offenders, and the halls of residence were filled with student actors. It made for a very real scenario.

For the university registrar, it was a wake-up call. Within minutes of the exercise starting, he was told that there were three media helicopters flying over the campus; that the offenders had set up video cameras within the halls, which were streaming live feeds onto the internet; and that the university's phone-lines were jammed with incoming calls as news of the attacks spread. He had 15,000 people on campus and few means of communication to tell them what to do.

After several hours of working through the scenario, the exercise was rounded out with two very moving talks: one from a student who had been at Virginia Tech at the time of its tragic shootings, and another from a visiting lecturer from Virginia Tech – both giving their impressions of how Virginia Tech had handled the massacre, which left 32 people dead.[18] These talks created an emotional impact – bringing home for the senior management team just how important it is to manage such a crisis well. That exercise was a turning point for the university; never again did the senior management team think that emergency management was a task to be delegated and forgotten. From that day forward, it became the senior management team asking when their next exercise would be.

In general, crisis planning is only taken seriously by leaders with prior crisis experience or within communities that have an emergency subculture born of previous disasters. If in your organization you don't have leaders already focused on being prepared for crises, then your first task is capture both their hearts and their minds on the need to become crisis ready. For the University of Canterbury, the Active Shooter exercise was so effective because it addressed these two elements effectively: the exercise itself illustrated the rational reasons for improving the university's response capability, but it was the presentations from those who had experienced a similar crisis that made them *want* to become better prepared.

Your organization's leadership also needs depth. While much of this discussion so far has focused on the senior leaders at the top of an organization, it is not just leadership at the top of the organization that is important. Good leadership skills are required throughout the organization. Large organizations are highly complex adaptive systems – senior leadership teams rarely have direct influence over everything that the organization does.

Following the Christchurch earthquakes in New Zealand, Nilakant and Bernard Walker led a research team exploring the nature of leadership that emerged within critical infrastructure organizations.[19] What they discovered was that how engaged staff felt to the organization after the earthquakes depended far more on the leadership qualities of their one-up manager than on the leadership decisions made at the top of the organization. In some cases, even though the organization was implementing the right sort of policies to support its staff during the crisis, if a staff member's line manager wasn't particularly great in emotional intelligence (EQ), staff felt disconnected from the organization as a whole.

It is important to spend time, both pre-crisis and during a crisis, supporting managers to be the best leaders that they can be. This also needs to be coupled with mechanisms for identifying managers who aren't providing good leadership to their staff, and diagnosing how that can be addressed. Leaving poor leaders in place not only prevents good organizational performance during business-as-usual, it also leaves an organization vulnerable to pockets of staff feeling disempowered, disengaged and more likely to leave the organization following times of crisis.

Provide the right leadership for the time

Many people talk about the need for decisive command-and-control leadership in times of crisis, but, in reality, this leadership style has limited effectiveness. Leadership needs evolve depending on the stage the organization is at (pre-crisis, at the height of crisis, or during recovery), and leaders need to evolve their style to meet these changing requirements.

Step back for a moment and reflect on what sort of leadership style you naturally exhibit. Each of us has a different style, and there is no one leadership style that is perfect from a resilience perspective. It's a matter of understanding what the strengths and weaknesses of your style are for particular situations, and making sure that you can adapt as required.

Leadership style matters, and, as Daniel Goleman discovered, it also has a measurable influence on business performance.[20] Good leaders don't rely on just one style of leadership, but have a suite of styles that they can draw on as the situation dictates:

Come with me leadership – mobilizing people towards a vision	One of the most effective leadership styles, both during times of crisis *and* in business-as-usual. It does require the leader to have a clear vision, however, of what is required. If this is missing, utilize the 'what do you think?' style to help develop that vision first.
People come first leadership – creating emotional bonds and support	This is a leadership style that demonstrates empathy and genuine concern for people. Used well, it boosts morale and engenders strong loyalty. This is a very important style for when people are themselves in crisis. The challenge comes when what is best for the business doesn't necessarily align with what is best for individuals.
What do you think leadership – building consensus through participation	This leadership style requires skills in listening. It has benefits in that people involved in a decision are more likely to 'buy into' that decision. Decision making is also improved by getting multiple perspectives. There is a risk, though, of too many meetings and taking too long to make decisions, so consider time-bounding the discussion to keep a balance between speed and consensus.
Lead by example leadership – setting high performance standards, expecting excellence and self-direction	Setting stretch-targets for people, to encourage them to achieve more than they ever thought possible, can be very powerful. Used alone, however, this leadership style can be overwhelming and demotivating, particularly if the leader starts micro-managing in order to ensure those targets are met. Used sparingly and coupled with coaching and affirmative leadership styles, however, leading by example can deliver exceptional results.

Coaching leadership – developing people for the future	This leadership style aims to bring out the best in your organization's greatest asset – its people. With a predominant focus on personal development rather than delivery, this leadership style delivers resilience over the longer term. To learn, we sometimes need to make mistakes. This style doesn't work well in high-pressure situations where mistakes can have disastrous consequences, unless there is some sort of safety net in place so that poor decisions or actions are remedied before they cause harm.
'Do this' leadership – requiring immediate compliance	This leadership style is often described as a 'command and control' type of approach. It can be very useful during the initial stages of a crisis if people are like deer in the headlights and urgent action is required. It should only be used in very small doses. People don't tend to like being ordered around, and, used too often, this leadership style can be detrimental to organizational performance.

Resilient leadership requires a measure of each of the above styles: a small measure of 'do this' leadership during the very initial stages of a crisis to get response started, equal portions of 'people come first', 'what do you think?' and 'coaching' leadership styles to bring out the best in your people and to ensure robust decisions. Add to this mix a small measure of 'leading by example' to create stretch-targets and achieve excellence. The largest measure, however, should be of 'come with me' leadership, bringing people with you through creating a vision of how your organization can and will get through this.

Summary

Here are some key take-outs from this chapter:

- To be a good leader is more than just filling a leadership role – it requires demonstrating leadership.
- Be clear in what you stand for and hold true to those core values.
- For people to want to follow you requires creating a sense of hope, painting a vision of what a better future could be.

- Focus on the people you are leading – find ways to be present and accessible for them.

- One person cannot do it alone – build your team and inspire good leadership from others.

- There is no one perfect way to be a resilient leader – a good leader must adapt their style as needs change.

Quick Start Guide: Leading in a crisis

When your organization is in the midst of crisis, use these prompts as a regular touchstone to reflect if you are delivering the leadership needed to get your organization through:

Do not try to lead on your own.	Draw on a leadership team of people that you can trust. Seek out multiple perspectives and be sure to stress-test key decisions.
Create an elevator speech of what you want to achieve.	Clearly articulate what it is that you want to achieve during the crisis and what the key priorities are. Get people inspired about what they can achieve.
Maintain a strategic focus.	Do not get drawn into micro-managing the operational response to a crisis. The more that you get buried in the detail, the less you can lead.
Stay true to your core values.	Think about what is really important for you and your organization and make sure that these do not get thrown out of the window just because you are in the heat of a crisis.
Lead from the heart as well as the head.	People need to know that you care about them and are committed to supporting them. Be present and available so that people know that you are there to lead them.
Reach out to others.	Utilize your networks, your colleagues and your friends as your support network so that they can help you through your time of crisis. You would do the same for them if it was their crisis.

Resilience initiatives – building resilient leadership

At the end of this book are a number of different initiatives that organizations can to use to improve their resilience. The initiatives with particular relevance for building resilient leadership are numbers:

11 Self-evaluate and actively improve your own leadership skills.

12 Exercise strategic dilemmas.

13 Capture both hearts and minds.

14 Build the leadership skills of junior and middle leaders.

15 Empower your staff to lead during a crisis.

16 Build a crisis leadership team.

43 Practise decision making without all the information.

56 Develop good decision-making practices.

58 Have good succession planning.

63 Make resilience an organizational goal.

64 Embed core values in day-to-day operations.

66 Maintain a strategic focus.

References and further reading

A good way to find copies of academic papers is via Google Scholar: https://scholar.google.com.

1 All Blacks rugby team:
  - Johnson, T, Martin, AJ, Palmer, F *et al* (2012) Collective leadership: A case study of the All Blacks, *Asia-Pacific Management and Business Application*, **1** (1), pp 53–67
  - Howitt, B (2012) *Graham Henry: Final word*, Harper Sport, Auckland
  - Chirichello, M (2001) Collective leadership: sharing the principalship, *Principal*, **81** (1), pp 46, 48, 50–51

2 Bernardo, S (2010) An interview with Admiral Thad Allen: you have to lead from everywhere, *Harvard Business Review*, **88** (11)

3 Tylenol tampering:
  - Moore, T (1982) The fight to save Tylenol, *Fortune*, **106** (11), pp 44–49, http://fortune.com/2012/10/07/the-fight-to-save-tylenol-fortune-1982/

- Fulmer, RM and Goldsmith, M (2001) *The Leadership Investment: How the world's best organizations gain strategic advantage through leadership development*, AMACOM Div American Mgmt Assn, New York
- Sonenshein, S (2005) Business ethics and internal social criticism, *Business Ethics Quarterly*, **15** (3), pp 475–98
- Rehak, J (2002) Tylenol made a hero of Johnson & Johnson: the recall that started them all, *The New York Times*, 23 March, http://www.nytimes.com/2002/03/23/your-money/23iht-mjj_ed3_.html

4 Johnson and Johnson (nd) Our Credo Values, Johnson and Johnson, http://www.jnj.com/about-jnj/jnj-credo/

5 *Exxon Valdez*:

- Williams, DE and Treadaway, G (1992) Exxon and the Valdez accident: A failure in crisis communication, *Communication Studies*, **43** (1), pp 56–64
- Holusha, J (1989) Exxon's public relations problem, *The New York Times*, 21 April, http://www.nytimes.com/1989/04/21/business/exxon-s-public-relations-problem.html?pagewanted=all
- Williams, DE and Olaniran, BA (1994) Exxon's decision-making flaws: the hypervigilant response to the Valdez grounding, *Public Relations Review*, **20** (1), pp 5–18
- Garcia, HF (2006) Effective leadership response to crisis, *Strategy & Leadership*, **34** (1), pp 4–10
- Forman, JP and Ross, LA (2013) *Integral Leadership: The next half-step*, SUNY Press, Albany, NY

6 Ford and Firestone:

- Garcia, HF (2006) Effective leadership response to crisis, *Strategy & Leadership*, **34** (1), pp 4–10
- Moll, R (2003) Ford Motor Company and the Firestone tyre recall, *Journal of Public Affairs*, **3** (3), pp 200–11
- Biggemann, S and Buttle, F (2007) The Ford Explorer–Firestone tires crisis: a rules theory analysis of relationships, in *23rd Industrial Marketing and Purchasing Group Conference. Exploiting the B2B Knowledge Network: New Perspectives and Core Concepts*, Manchester

7 Toyota unintended acceleration:

- Heller, VL and Darling, JR (2012) Anatomy of crisis management: lessons from the infamous Toyota case, *European Business Review*, **24** (2), pp 151–68

8 Volkswagen fuel emissions:

- Ewing, J (2016) Volkswagen inquiry expands to 17 suspects, *The New York Times*, 8 March, http://www.nytimes.com/2016/03/09/business/international/volkswagen-inquiry-germany.html?_r=2

– Gates, G, Ewing, J, Russell, K *et al* (2016) Explaining Volkswagen's emissions scandal, *The New York Times*, 1 June, http://www.nytimes.com/ interactive/2015/business/international/vw-diesel-emissions-scandal-explained. html

9 Kay, R and Goldspink, C (2012) *CEO Perspectives on Resilience*, Australian Government, http://www.tisn.gov.au/Documents/Research%20paper%201%20 -%20CEO%20perspectives%20on%20organisational%20resilience.pdf

10 Mississippi Power case study:

– Cauchon, D (2015) The little company that could, *USA Today*, 9 October, http://usatoday30.usatoday.com/money/companies/management/2005-10-09-mississippi-power-usat_x.htm

– Mississippi Power (2014) *Hurricane Katrina: The Mississippi Power story*, YouTube, https://www.youtube.com/watch?v=4fzvFVoLZrU

– Simmons, D (2007) Mississippi Power: always on. *National Organisational Resilience Framework Workshop*, Mt Macedon, Australia, 5–7 December

– Ratcliff, D (2005) *Testimony of David Ratcliffe, President and CEO, Southern Company*, Senate Committee on Homeland Security and Governmental Affairs, 16 November 16

11 Cauchon, D (2015) The little company that could, *USA Today*, 9 October, http://usatoday30.usatoday.com/money/companies/management/2005-10-09-mississippi-power-usat_x.htm

12 Rudolf Giuliani's leadership through the 9/11 attacks:

– Giuliani, RW and Kurson, K (2002) *Leadership*, Miramax Books, New York

– Powell, M (2007) In 9/11 chaos, Giuliani forged a lasting image, *The New York Times*, 21 September, http://www.nytimes.com/2007/09/21/us/ politics/21giuliani.html?_r=1

– Puente, S, Crous, F and Venter, A (2007) The role of a positive trigger event in actioning authentic leadership development, *SA Journal of Human Resource Management*, 5 (1), pp 11–18

– Lubar, K and Halpern, BL (2004) *Leadership Presence*, Penguin, New York

– Forbes, S (2011) Remembering 9/11: the Rudy Giuliani interview, *Forbes*, 9 September, http://www.forbes.com/sites/steveforbes/2011/09/09/ remembering-911-the-rudy-giuliani-interview/#2715e4857a0b44e37bf65897

– Sylves, R (2008) *Disaster Policy and Politics: Emergency management and homeland security*, Sage, Thousand Oaks, CA

13 Giuliani, RW and Kurson, K (2002) *Leadership*, Miramax Books, New York

14 Boin, A and 'tHart, P (2003) Public leadership in times of crisis: mission impossible? *Public Administration Review*, **63** (5), pp 544–53

15 Ford, D (1985) *The Button. The Nuclear Trigger: Does it work?* Allen & Unwin, London

16 Carrel, LF (2000) Training civil servants for crisis management, *Journal of Contingencies and Crisis Management*, **8** (4), pp 192–96

17 Two books that provide further insights into the University of Canterbury's emergency preparedness and what helped them to recover from the Canterbury earthquakes are:

– Seville, E, Hawker, C and Lyttle, J (2012) *Resilience Tested: A year and a half of 10,000 aftershocks*, University of Canterbury, http://www.canterbury.ac.nz/emergency/documents/resiliencetested.pdf

– Seville, E, Hawker, C and Lyttle, J (2011) *Shaken but Not Stirred: A university's resilience in the face of adversity*, University of Canterbury, http://www.canterbury.ac.nz/emergency/documents/shakenbutnotstirred.pdf

18 Virginia Tech (nd) *We Remember*, https://www.weremember.vt.edu/

19 Nilakant, V, Walker, B and Rochford, K (2013) *Post-disaster Management of Human Resources: Learning from an extended crisis*, Resilient Organisations Research Report2013/03, http://www.resorgs.org.nz/images/stories/pdfs/OrganisationalResilience/post_disaster_management_of_human_resources.pdf

20 Goleman, D (2000) Leadership that gets results, *Harvard Business Review*, March–April

Staff engagement – having a team of engaged people

03

Mary, a nurse in the intensive care unit at a major city hospital, is afraid. She has a decision to make – should she go to work today? Her husband pleads with her to call in sick. As the mother of three small children, he asks, how could she put them at risk? If she goes to work, she will have to care for patients infected by the outbreak. Mary is torn. She feels her primary responsibility is to protect her children, but at the same time, she has a strong sense of duty and wants to support her workmates on the front lines. What should she do?

In early 2003, Mary's decision was faced by thousands of healthcare workers in China, Hong Kong, Canada, Taiwan, Singapore and Vietnam. When SARS first flashed around the world, there was very little known about the disease.[1] What we did know was that it was highly infectious and killed one in 10 people infected. For older people it was even more deadly – nearly half of those aged over 65 died from the disease.[2]

At the time of the outbreak, no one really knew how SARS was spread, how long it could survive, or for how long people were contagious. Our society was on the brink of a major pandemic, and healthcare workers treating those infected were quickly becoming victims themselves. In Canada, 43 per cent of SARS cases were healthcare workers.[3] Even to this day there are still no known cures or vaccinations for SARS.

So did healthcare workers turn up to work? Overwhelmingly, around the world the answer was yes. While there were reports of some physicians and nurses refusing to work with suspected SARS patients, overall this was not a significant problem. Some managers in fact found the greater problem was convincing healthcare workers to stay home if they had any SARS symptoms – many healthcare workers with mild symptoms reported to the hospital anyway.

For Mary, in making her decision to go into work that day or not, she had to weigh up conflicting priorities – between family and work. In this chapter we'll explore why people come to work and give their all during times of adversity, and how your organization can work to tip those scales in your favour.

Just because your organization may not be a healthcare provider doesn't mean that Mary's dilemma isn't relevant. Whenever a crisis strikes, of any kind, there are going to be tough times ahead. In many instances the crisis response phase is 'heroic' – everyone pitches in and there is a strong sense of camaraderie. As the initial rush of adrenalin passes though, things often take a turn for the worse. Recovery can be a long hard slog. If people see that they are no longer getting back from their work what they are putting into it, they will start to leave – just at the time when you need them most.

Organizations really do need their people. When groups are put under pressure, it is their people and how they come together that can make or break an organization.

For me, this was illustrated as we tracked businesses recovering from the earthquakes in Christchurch. Across the city, businesses faced damaged buildings, wrecked machinery, destroyed stock, broken infrastructure and inaccessible neighbourhoods. Even in the face of all this physical damage, businesses consistently told us that it was the people aspects of the disaster that they found most challenging.

So if people are such an important ingredient in your organization's resilience, how do you know if the team that you have in place has what it takes? Here are some questions to ponder (Figure 3.1):

How *competent* are your people to perform in environments of rapid change and uncertainty?

Are your people *committed* enough to go the extra mile to get things done?

Do your people work well together as a *connected* team?

Are your people well *supported*, pulling together when things get hard?

If your answer to any of the above questions is 'maybe not', your organization has some work to do. Having good people and getting the best out of them, particularly during times of great stress, is not something that happens overnight, but when it does, magic can happen.

Figure 3.1 Building blocks for developing an engaged team

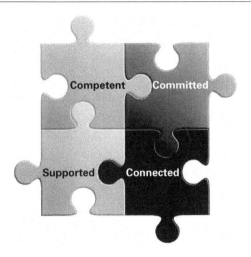

Competent – skilled, practised and ready to improvise

Debbie Van Opstal from the US Resilience Project[4] has a wonderful metaphor for explaining the importance of competence. She describes it like being able to play jazz. Jazz music is the ultimate in improvisation – each musician feeds off the others in a complex and adaptive way. The result can either be a discordant mess or pure genius. To get great jazz requires the musicians to have a very high level of competence – they can't improvise if they are still struggling with the basics.

I love this example because it sums up what you are looking for in competent employees. You want them not only to be able to do their task, but to also feel sufficiently confident in their roles that they can divert off-script if they need to. You want them to have a broad operational picture, so if the way they 'normally' do things isn't possible, they have sufficient know-how, confidence and insight to find a different way to get it achieved.

You don't need to wait for a crisis, though, to develop your team's competence for dealing with the unexpected. If there are common situations likely to arise in many crises your organization might face, identify them and practise your response.

Military personnel, as part of their weapon familiarization training, are taught to strip down and then reassemble their guns. Each step is broken down into simple movements and repeated over and over again. With repetition they progressively become faster and faster. Once they are proficient, they then move on to practising doing it blindfolded. Eventually, putting your gun together becomes a bit like touch-typing. You don't need to think about where the letters are on your keyboard – you just know.

We all have instinctive responses that kick in when we sense danger.[5] Our body reacts by sending out cortisol hormones, which act as a siren, alerting every part of your body to the threat. As you prepare for fight or flight, your heart starts to beat faster, your blood pressure increases, you breathe faster and your liver releases more sugar into your blood. Your body is ready for action.

Your mind also prepares to respond. When in survival mode, your mind becomes sharper so your instinctive reactions get faster. To compensate, however, your mind's zone of focus narrows. This means that your ability to collate multiple sources of information diminishes markedly and your ability to think through complex problems reduces.

Knowing this, there are some key steps you need to take to prepare your team for dealing with crises. During the very initial stages of a response, the actions people take need to be instinctive. Why do we have regular fire alarm drills? They prime the brain to associate the sound of the fire alarm with the right set of response actions (and, along the way, to test if there are any unforeseen problems in implementing those actions – such as blocked exits, overcrowded stairwells etc). These drills help to make the response to evacuate instinctive. Complex thinking about what the alarm means and how to respond is no longer required – you know that the correct response is to evacuate. It becomes automatic, just like being able to assemble a weapon blindfolded.

You cannot script how to manage every part of a crisis, but it is important to plan and practise (over and over again) the initial responses needed during high-stakes situations. The very start of a response is when the cortisol hormone is charging around the body. People will be in a high-adrenalin state, and are therefore less able to think.

At the very least, your team needs to be practised in how to activate a crisis response. If, for your organization, that involves notifying executives to get them on a crisis call, or to meet somewhere, or to take some other action – make sure you drill this at least four times a year. Do it at different times of the day, with different permutations of challenges they have to overcome (such as the conference call facility isn't working, or the premises are inaccessible), but above all do it regularly! Also consider ways to lighten the 'thinking load' for people during the early response phase, for example by using checklists to ensure that key steps are not missed.

There will be situations, however, where you don't have the luxury of being able to buy yourself time before complex decisions need to be made. For example, while police will generally try to slow down a hostage situation so that negotiations can be undertaken in a calmer state of mind, that isn't always possible. Sometimes, the complex decisions come when you are least capable of making them.

You can prepare people for these kinds of situation through war-gaming-type exercises. These types of situation feel very real and give people practice at having to think while experiencing the rush of adrenalin. Practising how a scenario might play out lets people become familiar with how they are instinctively likely to feel and react, and the types of response they need to guard against. Debriefing following each game allows people to think about whether their response was the right one, and if things went terribly wrong, other ways they might potentially have played it. War-gaming needs to be realistic to get the players really experiencing a biochemical response. It will also make for a highly memorable experience – and one that the body can instinctively pattern-match to, if a real event occurs that is similar.

There are two other very important techniques that you can use for dealing with complex problems in high-adrenalin situations. The first is to try to lower the adrenalin. This can be very challenging to do – but there is real value in teaching people the importance of taking a moment to '*pause, reflect and breathe*'. The second is to consider the environment that teams are working in. Are they busy, noisy places? If you have teams that are dealing with particularly complex problems, try to get them away from the buzz of a response. Do they really need the distraction of minute-by-minute updates on the situation? Have them work from elsewhere, where they can think better.

In 1970, NASA was attempting a third manned mission to the moon.[6] Two days after the Apollo 13 spacecraft set off, however, disaster stuck. The astronauts heard a sharp bang and felt a vibration. With warning lights blinking, one oxygen tank appeared to be completely empty and there were indications that the oxygen in the second tank was rapidly depleting. The potential catastrophe was confirmed when, looking out of the window, Commander Jim Lovell observed: 'We are venting something out into the… into space… It's a gas of some sort.' It was oxygen gas escaping from the second, and last, oxygen tank.

The command module's normal supply of electricity, light and water was lost, and they were a long way from Earth. Without a source of heat, cabin temperatures quickly dropped down close to freezing. Since oxygen fed the spacecraft's fuel cells, power was reduced as well. The crew retreated from the main command module into the smaller lunar module. The crew rationed water, but their bigger challenge was how to keep carbon dioxide at non-toxic levels.

There were enough lithium hydroxide canisters on board to remove carbon dioxide from the spacecraft, but the square canisters from the command module were not compatible with the round openings in the lunar module environmental system. After a day and a half in the lunar module, a warning light showed that carbon dioxide levels were rising dangerously.

I always remember the scene in the Apollo 13 movie where they pulled together a small team and led them away from Mission Control. They put this team into a small, windowless room and tasked them with finding a way to fit new air-filters into the lunar module. With a load of spare parts dumped on the table (all that the astronauts had on the shuttle), the team were given 24 hours to come up with a solution. Using plastic bags, cardboard and tape, they managed to find a way to get a square air-filter to fit into a round hole, so that the astronauts could survive the journey back home.

There is a good reason that this team was removed from the busy main Mission Control room – they needed to think, and to do that they needed to be in a conducive environment.

Three days after the major Christchurch earthquake, the University of Canterbury moved its entire executive team away from the emergency operations centre, and into a building that was 10 minutes' walk away. Again, this was done for a reason. The university needed to lower the adrenalin state of their most senior managers, so that they could move beyond thinking about the immediate problems they faced, to consider more strategically how they were going to recover the university over the longer term.

A further technique you can use to improve the competence of your team during high-stakes situations is to try to make the 'unusual' more 'usual'.

An electricity lines company doesn't normally feed or provide accommodation for 10,000 people at short notice. But during Hurricane Katrina, this is exactly the challenge that Mississippi Power faced as it brought in crews from right around the United States to help it to get the power back on.[7] With a bit of forethought and planning, Mississippi Power had found ways to create this capability. People knew what to do, and had prepared for the role they needed to play.

Mississippi Power is a small organization of only about 1,200 employees. Being a small organization, it knows that it doesn't have sufficient resources internally to be able to respond to every hurricane alone. Instead, it has developed a simple and yet elegant solution for both making the most of the resources it does have, and for bringing in help when required.

Mississippi Power has a well-developed programme of mutual aid agreements with other power companies from around the United States, which it utilizes on a regular basis. Using and practising the deployment of these mutual aid agreements regularly, rather than seeing them as a measure of last resort, means that the company has become highly skilled at integrating and supporting out-of-state crews.

Everyone, from the CEO to the person who answers the phones, knows what their role is during a crisis. For example, the marketing department knows that its role during a crisis is to provide accommodation, catering and facilities for out-of-state crews. Following Hurricane Katrina, this team catered for more than 10,000 people, which is no mean feat in the midst of a disaster zone. They also plan for how to support the families of staff who can't get home because they are working long hours, forming family support teams to help clean up damaged homes and care for relatives. The entire organization mobilizes to support its mission of getting the power back on to affected communities.

The reason it was able to do all this is that staff knew in advance what they needed to do – they had actively prepared for it.

Committed – people enabled to be part of the solution

The other day, a friend was describing how she felt about her current employer, and it summed up employee engagement perfectly. She said: 'I love my job – I love what we do; I love the part that I play in it; I love that I can make a difference. And because of that I will go out of my way to do whatever I can to make us successful. I would even ask my Mum to help if I thought it was useful. I have been part of organizations before, but have never felt committed enough to draw on my own personal networks for them.'

Engaged employees invest their physical, cognitive and emotional energy into their work. They will contribute to your organization with their hands, their head and their heart. Employee engagement is not just another term for job satisfaction – you can be satisfied with your job without being enamoured of your employer. An engaged employee will go above and beyond their job description, putting in discretionary effort to help the organization achieve its goals – and they will do so willingly.

Employee engagement[8] has received increasing interest over the past decade, from both academics and practitioners. While there has been much discovered, we also still have much to learn. There remains debate over exactly what employee engagement is, how it should be measured, what conditions lead to employee engagement, and what the outcomes of employee engagement are.

Different researchers have different models that they use to describe the factors that lead to employee engagement, but common themes include:

- the extent to which an employee understands their role and has the capability and capacity to deliver on it;
- how important the employee perceives the vision or mission of the organization to be, and the extent to which they can see how their role contributes to that;
- the extent to which the employee feels their work is recognized and valued; and
- the nature of relationships they have with others in the workplace, and the extent to which they feel both supported and challenged to grow and develop through their work.

In other words, people need to be competent, committed, connected and supported – the same things needed to support the resilience of your organization. But engagement isn't something that is only important during times of crisis – studies have also found that employee engagement is also linked to better organizational performance. For example, one meta-study (which is a study that draws together the findings from multiple other studies) computed a composite performance metric for 7,939 business units. These performance metrics were based on a combination of financial performance, customer satisfaction and employee turnover. They then compared each business unit's performance score with its employee engagement to see if there was any relationship. They discovered that organizations with above average employee engagement had an average performance success rating of 63 per cent, compared to just 37 per cent for business units with below-average employee engagement.[9]

Air New Zealand won the Oscar of the airline industry, Air Transport World's 'Airline of the Year Award', in both 2010 and 2012. But life for the airline hasn't always been so rosy.[10]

Like Swiss Air, the week of the 11 September terrorist attacks was not a good one for Air New Zealand. Again, the source of its problems was not just terror attacks; it had also made unwise investments in other airlines. Air New Zealand had recently purchased an Australian airline, Ansett Australia, and soon found itself haemorrhaging money at a rate of $1.3 million a day.

On 14 September 2001, Ansett Australia collapsed and nearly brought Air New Zealand down with it. Air New Zealand was just 20 minutes away from being declared bankrupt when the New Zealand government bailed it out to the tune of $870 million. The injection of cash alone, however, was never going to solve Air New Zealand's problems. Air New Zealand had a workforce that had lost its confidence and few obvious competitive advantages to draw on.

Rob Fyfe was tasked with finding a strategy that would start the airline on a journey towards recovery. Rob was new to the organization, having recently been appointed as chief information officer. Looking around, the only thing Rob could identify as a potential strategic advantage for Air New Zealand was its New Zealand-ness.

Through numerous focus groups with international visitors, Rob and his team realized that it wasn't just New Zealand's spectacular beauty that visitors valued – they consistently talked about the friendly, down-to-earth openness of the New Zealand people. So, they decided to create an airline built on the authenticity and personality of its people.

Later, when Rob was promoted to CEO, he discarded words such as 'vision, mission and strategy' and instead set about telling stories that brought to life how people make an organization. All 11,500 employees were handed the opportunity, and responsibility, to be themselves and to engage with colleagues, customers and suppliers in a genuine and engaging Kiwi manner.

The philosophies 'be yourself', 'welcome as a friend', 'can do' and 'share your New Zealand' started to permeate everything within the organization. It also ultimately shaped the airline's reputation in the marketplace.

Rob practised what he preached. As CEO, he made a point of personally meeting every single new recruit to the organization (of which there are more than a thousand each year). He also personally responded to every customer letter of compliment or complaint, and shared them openly with all employees, so they could see the direct impact their attitudes and behaviours were having on the customer experience.

Through his intentional approach to creating a culture and a 'personality' within Air New Zealand that allowed employees to feel trusted, supported and empowered to be themselves, Air New Zealand turned its fortunes around.

In Rob Fyfe's words: 'Today 88.9% of our staff feel genuinely connected with the company, compared with 68.5% three years ago. Our reputation in the marketplace helps build staff culture and vice versa, and customer service levels correlate closely with the increased sense of engagement and connection'.[11]

It is this sort of engagement that won Air New Zealand the Airline of the Year Award in 2010, just nine years after beginning the journey to recovery.

Connected – when the whole is greater than the sum of the parts

No one person can ever know the complete answer to a complex problem. Bringing together people with different areas of expertise, experience and background is key to managing crises effectively. By collaborating, we get to a solution quicker, and often with more elegance.

Dave Parsons spent many years working in the water sector in Australia. The water sector, like many others, is faced with an ageing workforce and increasing churn, as employees switch roles and companies more often. Dave used the concept of 3G (three-generational) teams to capture the opportunity that comes from the diverse teams he works with.

Working with him, Dave had people with a wealth of experience – they had been with the organization for many years and just 'know' how things work. Because they have been around for a long time, they remember why the system was configured in certain ways, understand its quirks and nuances, and have a very good overview of the network and how it all fits together. These people know things that aren't part of the formal knowledge base of the organization.

There are also people who might be fairly new to the organization, but they bring with them significant experience from working in a different industry, or they may have worked with other organizations in the water sector. These people bring new perspectives on how things can be done – ideas that have worked elsewhere.

There are also the younger staff who see the world in different ways from their older colleagues. They are tech savvy, live in a world of social media, and while they may not have a wealth of experience to call on, they are refreshingly free of blinkers as to how things can (or should) be done.

In a crisis, we need diversity of perspectives for the best ideas to emerge. The concept of '3G teams' is to purposefully bring diverse perspectives together for creatively solving problems by ensuring that all generations are represented in every team. Each of the above cohorts, on its own, has gaps in its capability. But together, they make for a powerful team.

When talking with Dave about how these 3G teams work in practice, he says it is often the little things that make the difference. For example, during one flooding event, senior engineers were using maps of the city to explain where the flood waters were currently at and which bits of critical infrastructure had been affected. Seeing that people were struggling to visualize exactly what had been impacted, one of young staff jumped onto Google Maps; using Street View, he placed himself at the edge of the water line and took a virtual walk around the edge of the flooding. For the young staff member, there was nothing special in what he did – he used technology such as Street View all the time as part of everyday life. But instantly, the task of communicating the extent of the problem had become a whole lot easier. People could see which buildings already had floodwaters through them, and which would likely be flooded next.

What I love about the 3G teams example is that it ticks so many boxes. 3G teams have great business-as-usual benefits. They help to up-skill younger staff by having them work actively alongside senior staff. 3G teams also help to share tacit knowledge that is held by the senior staff, passing it down to the next generation. A side benefit is that it works wonders for the organization's resilience – increasing the capacity for creative problem solving of all involved.

Being connected and working together well is important for managing the inevitable surge in workload that accompanies times of rapid change and crisis. Resilient organizations have a 'one-in–all-in' attitude to crises. People from right across the organization will pitch in to help those who are most affected.

As you are reading this, I bet you are thinking how obvious it is that a whole-of-organization response is needed during a crisis. And yet we see, time and time again, situations where one department is struggling to cope with a major issue that is unfolding around it, while the rest of the organization continues on oblivious.

For your organization, have a think about how well different parts of your organization work together. Does your organization play as 'one team'? If you don't see this happening during normal business, don't expect your organization to suddenly come together to play as one team during times of crisis. This capability needs to be developed and practised. Regularly use cross-organization teams to solve business-as-usual problems. Change your office layout to create a work environment that brings people together. Design key performance indicators (KPIs) to reward collaboration and positive behaviours. The ways you can create better connections within your organization are endless.

Social networks matter for performance. Gathering together data from 37 different studies, researchers analysed the data collected on more than 3,000 teams, ranging from teams working together on a production line and senior executive teams in large corporations, through to teams in the military. Teams with a denser network of connections between team members were more likely to attain their goals and also more likely to stay together over the longer term.[12]

It isn't just work- or task-related connections (such as whether someone has worked with someone else before) that are important. Social connections or friendships are also important. In fact, both work and social connections had similar levels of influence on team performance. A greater level of social connection had the added benefit of supporting team viability – how long a team stays together.

Having a team of people who know each other, care about each other and work well together isn't just about delivering great performance. From a resilience perspective, people that feel supported are also better able to deal with conditions of extreme stress and uncertainty.

Supported – helping people to remain personally resilient

We all know that some individuals get through life's hurdles more easily than others. Psychologists have been researching for many years what makes some individuals more resilient than others.[13]

In the 1990s, researchers looked at children who were thriving, despite their high-risk circumstances. Many of these children were being maltreated, exposed to violence or had parents with severe mental illness, and yet they were doing OK. Researchers began to ponder what gave them their inner strength and capability to adapt that enabled them to transcend their circumstances. They came up with a number of different traits contributing to the resilience of these children: their autonomy, their self-esteem, their internal locus of control (the extent to which they believe they can influence the circumstances that affect them), and their self-efficacy (their own belief in their ability to reach their goals). Over time, other traits such as optimism and self-determination (the extent to which their actions are of their own choosing) have also been identified as enhancing resilience.

In the early 2000s, this focus started to shift. Rather than seeing resilience as just an innate trait of an individual's personality, researchers started looking for ways to proactively develop resilience through various coping strategies that can help an individual to be more flexible and emotionally stable when presented with change. An example might be the rallying of support from friends, family and other support services that act as a buffer, softening the impact and maintaining a greater level of resilience.

For an organization, proactively seeking out people with both traits and coping strategies that support greater resilience can be a sound recruitment strategy. But just 'hiring more resilient people' is no guarantee that people will be resilient when you need them to be. People's level of resilience will naturally fluctuate over time. Major life events, such as a death in the family, marriage breakdown or loss of employment, can see people's resilience eroded; people who may have once been able to cope, suddenly become far more vulnerable to future shocks in their lives.

Following the Canterbury earthquakes, the Canterbury District Health Board and the Mental Health Foundation of New Zealand came together to help the people of the region to remain personally and collectively resilient.[14] They started a campaign called 'All Right?' which encouraged people living in Canterbury to focus on their wellbeing. The first phase of the campaign ran for six weeks and was all about 'normalizing the experience' – helping people to understand that the feelings they were experiencing are normal for anyone who has just experienced a major disaster. The second phase focused on 'checking in' – encouraging people to stop and consider their wellbeing and that of others, and to take small steps to address it. The third phase focused on 'community wellbeing' – providing opportunities and resources to help people come together while they improved their wellbeing. The latest phase in the campaign focused on 'emotional literacy' – making people aware that recovering from a disaster emotionally can take between five and 10 years, and that people are all at different places on their recovery journey. This wonderful campaign focuses on promoting long-term psychological wellbeing of the general population following disaster. It contains some really neat ideas that are directly applicable to any organization helping their people to recover from a major crisis.

At the heart of the All Right? campaign are five simple principles for improving wellbeing (described as the 5+ a day – a bit like the healthy eating guideline of eating 5+ a day of fruit and vegetables). The Five Ways to Wellbeing were identified by the UK government's Foresight Project on Mental Capital and Wellbeing.[15] This project extensively reviewed the best available scientific evidence to identify factors that influence an individual's mental development and wellbeing, from conception until death. From that research they came up with five simple actions that individuals do to proactively improve their wellbeing.

The Five Ways to Wellbeing are: to connect, to give, to take notice, to learn and to be active (Figure 3.2). These simple actions are something that anyone can do to improve their ability to cope with adversity.

Figure 3.2   The Five Ways to Wellbeing. Reproduced with permission from the Mental Health Foundation of New Zealand

The Mental Health Foundation of New Zealand has taken the concept of the Five Ways to Wellbeing and developed simple tools to help people to build them into everyday life. An example is the Wellbeing Game,[16] which is an app that activates the Five Ways in daily life, enabling lived experience of wellbeing. It encourages people to reflect and share what they have done each day to connect, give, take notice, learn or be active. Our researchers are now starting to explore the use of tools such as the Wellbeing Game within the workplace to improve organizational resilience.

Having people who are resilient does not automatically translate into having an organization or a team that is necessarily resilient, though they are related. The dynamics of how individuals come together and work together can create a group that is either more or less resilient than its members on their own. It is in this context that the idea of Employee Resilience (as a related but different concept from individual resilience) starts to emerge.

As individuals, we take cues from others around us as to how we should respond or behave. This can be either explicitly, through policies and practices that define 'the way we do things around here', through to implicit indicators of what types of behaviours and attitudes are and are not acceptable within a particular workplace. This means that depending on the culture your organization has, it can enhance or erode the resilience of all employees.

The Employee Resilience (EmpRes) research group at the University of Canterbury[17] describes employee resilience as employee capability, *facilitated and supported by the organization*, to utilize resources to continually adapt and flourish at work, even when faced with challenging circumstances. Their team has been working to develop a survey for evaluating the extent to which people engage in resilient behaviours within their work environment. The types of questions asked in the survey include how well people collaborate effectively with others to handle unexpected challenges; how they manage periods of high workload; how they resolve crises at work; how they learn from mistakes at work; how they seek to continually improve; how they respond to feedback at work; how they seek assistance at work; the approachability of managers; and the extent to which they see change at work as an opportunity for growth.

The Employee Resilience Scale is not designed to be used to evaluate the resilience of individuals; rather, it is designed to provide insight into behaviours and norms within the workplace that influence the resilience of people working within that environment. To find out more about how your organization is supporting employee resilience, see initiative 22 at the end of this book.

Summary

Here are some key take-outs from this chapter:

- When an organization is put under pressure, it is its people and how they come together that can make or break the organization.
- Adrenalin reduces our capacity for complex thinking – so it is important to plan and practise (over and over again) the initial responses needed during a crisis.
- Focus on improving employee engagement – an engaged employee will willingly go above and beyond their job description, putting in discretionary effort to help your organization.
- Having a team that is connected and works well together is important for managing the inevitable surge in workload that accompanies times of rapid change and crisis.
- Organizations can take proactive steps to improve the resilience of their employees by fostering a work culture that promotes resilient behaviours.

Quick Start Guide: Looking after your people in a crisis

When your organization is in the midst of crisis, it is important to demonstrate that you care. And not just with words, but also with actions and initiatives to support people as they negotiate the stressful situations that crises inevitably present. People want to know that you have their personal welfare at heart, and not just that of the organization:

Make contact.	Ensure you have plans for how you will contact people to make sure they are OK, to see what help they need, and to keep them informed.
Recognize that how a person experiences a situation is unique to them.	Don't assume how badly affected a person may be – it depends on so many complex factors.
Get a 360° perspective.	What else is going on in someone's life has a significant impact on how well they will cope with the current situation.
Keep asking.	Someone who was coping last week may be falling apart this week – keep tabs on how people are doing.
Demonstrate that you care.	This means demonstrating you care not just with words but also with attitudes, behaviours and actions.
Be fair and equitable.	Don't play favourites – try to ensure no parts of the organization are left behind.
Support middle-managers.	Your middle-managers need to be the best leaders they can be – it is through them that all your organization's efforts are translated.
Connect people.	Find ways to bring people and teams back together. If they can't meet at work, could they get together in other ways?
Understand that people will be at different stages.	Recovery is a roller coaster of ups and downs. Foster a culture that is accepting of wherever people are along that journey.

Don't underestimate the time and effort required. When planning for crises, organizations tend to forget to plan for their people. On the Resilient Organisation's website we have a free booklet with more advice on how to look after your people in an extended crisis: *Staffed or Stuffed.*[18]

Resilience initiatives – building engagement

At the end of this book are a number of different initiatives that organizations can use to improve their resilience. The initiatives with particular relevance for building a team of engaged people are:

17 Run a staff engagement survey.

18 Have dual job descriptions for staff.

19 Make work a place that staff want to come to.

20 Support the families of your staff.

21 Play the Wellbeing Game.

22 Review how well your organization is supporting employee resilience.

23 Engage staff in everyday business decisions and challenges.

42 Develop plans with your team.

49 Socialize your plans.

50 Map your staff vulnerabilities.

53 Make sure you can contact people.

54 Prepare key communications messages in advance.

63 Make resilience an organizational goal.

64 Embed core values in day-to-day operations.

65 Build a culture of optimism.

References and further reading

A good way to find copies of academic papers is via Google Scholar: https://scholar.google.com

1 SARS:
  - Singer, PA, Benatar, SR, Bernstein, M *et al* (2003) Ethics and SARS: lessons from Toronto, *BMJ: British Medical Journal*, **327** (7427), pp 1342–44
  - Lesperance, AM and Miller, JS (2009) *Preventing Absenteeism and Promoting Resilience Among Health Care Workers in Biological Emergencies*, Pacific Northwest National Laboratory, http://www.pnl.gov/main/publications/external/technical_reports/PNNL-18405.pdf
  - Straus, SE, Wilson, K, Rambaldini, G *et al* (2004) Severe acute respiratory syndrome and its impact on professionalism: qualitative study of physicians' behaviour during an emerging healthcare crisis, *BMJ: British Medical Journal*, **329** (7457), p 83, doi: 10.1136/bmj.38127.444838.63

2 World Health Organization (2003) *Update 49 – SARS case fatality ratio, incubation period*, World Health Organization, 7 May, http://www.who.int/csr/sarsarchive/2003_05_07a/en/

3 Tai, DY (2006) SARS: how to manage future outbreaks? *Annals, Academy of Medicine*, **35** (5), pp 368–73

4 The US Resilience Project aims to put the 'how-to' in resilience. On its website you can find reports and case studies that share best practices in building resilience from across the public and private sectors. See: http://usresilienceproject.org/

5 Physiological reactions to stress:
  - Sousa, DA (2009) *Brainwork*, Solution Tree Press, Bloomington, IN
  - Medina, J (2008) *Brain Rules: 12 principles for surviving and thriving at home, work, and school*, Pear Press, Edmonds, WA
  - NZ Defence Force (2002) *Developing Baseline: Building resilience*, New Zealand Defence Force, http://www.nzdf.mil.nz/downloads/pdf/force4families/Building-Resilience-Booklet.pdf

6 Apollo 13:
  - NASA (2009) *Apollo 13*, NASA, https://www.nasa.gov/mission_pages/apollo/missions/apollo13.html#.VrE32XkVipo
  - Howell, E (2012) *Apollo 13: Facts About NASA's near-disaster*, http://www.space.com/17250-apollo-13-facts.html
  - Howard, R (1995) *Apollo 13*, movie, Universal Pictures

7 Mississippi Power:
  - Cauchon, D (2005) The little company that could, *USA Today*, 9 October, http://usatoday30.usatoday.com/money/companies/management/2005-10-09-mississippi-power-usat_x.htm

- Mississippi Power (2014) *Hurricane Katrina: The Mississippi Power story*, YouTube, https://www.youtube.com/watch?v–4fzvFVoLZrU
- Simmons, D (2007) Mississippi Power: Always on, *National Organisational Resilience Framework Workshop*, Mt Macedon, Australia, 5–7 December
- Ratcliff, D (2005) *Testimony of David Ratcliffe, President and CEO, Southern Company*, Senate Committee on Homeland Security and Governmental Affairs, 16 November

8 Employee engagement:
- Rich, BL, Le Pine, JA and Crawford, ER (2010) Job engagement: antecedents and effects of job performance, *Academy of Management Journal*, **53**, pp 617–35
- Saks, AM and Gruman, JA (2014) What do we really know about employee engagement? *Human Resource Development Quarterly*, **25** (2), pp 155–82
- Kahn, WA (1990) Psychological conditions of personal engagement and disengagement at work, *Academy of Management Journal*, **33**, pp 692–724

9 Employee engagement and organizational outcomes:
- Harter, JK, Schmidt, FL and Hayes, TL (2002) Business-unit level relationship between employee satisfaction, employee engagement, and business outcomes, *Journal of Applied Psychology*, **87**, pp 268–79
- Harter, J, Schmidt, F, Agrawal, S *et al* (2012) *The Relationship Between Engagement at Work and Organizational Outcomes: 2012 Q12 meta-analysis*, Gallup, http://www.gallup.com/strategicconsulting/126806/q12-meta-analysis.aspx.

10 Air New Zealand:
- Birchfield, R (2010) Flying people not planes, *New Zealand Management*, **57** (8), pp 30–31
- Bradley, G (2013) Leaving Air NZ deputy chief still flying high, *New Zealand Herald*, 21 December, http://www.nzherald.co.nz/business/news/article.cfm?c_id–3&objectid–11176051
- Fyfe, R (2011) Leadership and Building a Culture of Innovation, presentation to the New Zealand Trade and Enterprise Better by Design CEO summit, http://idealog.co.nz/design/2011/03/rob-fyfe-leadership-and-building-culture-innovatio.

11 Birchfield, R (2010) Flying people not planes, *New Zealand Management*, **57** (8), pp 30–31

12 Social networks and team performance:
- Balkundi, P and Harrison, DA (2006) Ties, leaders, and time in teams: strong inference about network structure's effects on team viability and performance, *Academy of Management Journal*, **49** (1), pp 49–68
- Sparrowe, RT, Liden, RC, Wayne, SJ *et al* (2001) Social networks and the performance of individuals and groups, *Academy of Management Journal*, **44** (2), pp 316–25

- Kozlowski, SW and Ilgen, DR (2006) Enhancing the effectiveness of work groups and teams, *Psychological Science in the Public Interest*, **7** (3), pp 77–124

13 Individual resilience:

- Masten, AS, Best, KM and Garmezy, N (1990) Resilience and development: contributions from the study of children who overcome adversity, *Development and Psychopathology*, **2** (4), pp 425–44
- Benard, B (1995) *Fostering Resilience in Children*, ERIC Digest
- Näswall, K, Kuntz, J, Hodliffe, M *et al* (2013) *Employee Resilience Scale (EmpRes): Technical Report*, Resilient Organisations Research Report 2013/06, http://www.resorgs.org.nz/images/stories/pdfs/OrganisationalResilience/employee_resilience_scale.pdf
- Howard, S, Dryden, J and Johnson, B (1999) Childhood resilience: review and critique of literature, *Oxford Review of Education*, **25** (3), pp 307–23
- Wagnild, GM and Young, HM (1993) Development and psychometric evaluation of the Resilience Scale, *Journal of Nursing Measurement*, **1** (2), pp 165–78

14 For more information on the All Right? campaign and wellbeing take a look at the following websites – there are lots of free resources available to download: http://www.allright.org.nz/ and http://www.mentalhealth.org.nz/home/ways-to-wellbeing/

15 Foresight Mental Capital and Wellbeing Project (2008) *Foresight Mental Capital and Wellbeing Project: Final Project Report*, The Government Office for Science, London, https://www.gov.uk/government/uploads/system/uploads/attachment_data/file/292450/mental-capital-wellbeing-report.pdf

16 The Wellbeing Game:

- Mental Health Foundation of New Zealand (2015) https://www.thewellbeinggame.org.nz/
- Tonkins, K (2016) *Building Employee Resilience through Wellbeing in Organisations*, Master's thesis, University of Canterbury, http://www.resorgs.org.nz/Publications/building-employee-resilience-through-wellbeing-in-organisations.html

17 For more information on the Employee Resilience Scale, how it was developed and permissions for use, see:

- Employee Resilience (EmpRes) Research Programme, University of Canterbury, http://www.psyc.canterbury.ac.nz/research/empres/
- Näswall, K, Kuntz, J and Malinen, S (2015) *Employee Resilience Scale (EmpRes) Measurement Properties*, Resilient Organisations Research Report 2015/04, ISSN 1178-7279, http://www.resorgs.org.nz/Current-Research/employee-resilience.html

- Näswall, K, Kuntz, J, Hodliffe, M *et al* (2013) *Employee Resilience Scale (EmpRes): Technical Report*, Resilient Organisations Research Report 2013/06, http://www.resorgs.org.nz/images/stories/pdfs/OrganisationalResilience/employee_resilience_scale.pdf

- Tonkins, K (2016) *Building Employee Resilience through Wellbeing in Organisations*, Master's thesis, University of Canterbury, http://www.resorgs.org.nz/Publications/building-employee-resilience-through-wellbeing-in-organisations.html

18 Looking after your people in an extended crisis:

- Walker, B, Fraser, M and Nilakant, V (2014) *Staffed or Stuffed: Taking responsibility for your people in a major disaster*, Resilient Organisations Business Resource 2014/A, ISSN 2381-9790, http://www.resorgs.org.nz/staffed-or-stuffed.html

Social capital – having 3am friends

04

The 22 February earthquake in Christchurch struck at the worst possible time for the University of Canterbury (UC).[1] Not only was it during the middle of the day on a Tuesday, when the campus was teeming with staff and students, it was also Orientation Week – the first week of a new academic year.

For a university, Orientation Week is one of its most vulnerable times. UC had a whole intake of new students who were not yet bedded into the university environment – with few barriers to their transferring to another university. Other universities around New Zealand had not yet started teaching for the year, and were both willing and able to accept an influx of students fleeing the earthquakes in Christchurch. For UC, this was a nightmare proposition. Not only would they lose student enrolments for the 2011 year, but it would create a bow-wave effect of reduced student numbers for the next four years, as the depleted cohort of students progressed through their degrees.

UC was facing a financial black hole and needed to respond – quickly. The situation was bad. The campus was closed, with varying levels of damage to nearly all of their 240 buildings. Some buildings on campus would need to be demolished. The city had no potable drinking water. The sewage system was damaged and the city was being continuously rattled by major aftershocks. Students staying in the university halls of residence were told to go home and wait to hear when UC would reopen.

Parents around the country started to question whether it was wise to send their sons and daughters back to a city devastated by natural disaster. International students were particularly shaken by the news that 70 foreign students studying at an English language school in the city had been killed in a collapsed building. The risk of student flight was very real, and UC only had days to come up with a way to prevent it.

UC's response was innovative. It decided to 'help' students proactively to leave if they wanted to. But UC needed support from its friends to make this strategy possible.

Once students have gone to another university, for a semester or for a year, they are unlikely to return. They will have made new friends and started settling into their new courses and environments. To prevent this, UC had to find ways to maintain each student's connection and sense of identity as a UC student, even if he or she went somewhere else to study temporarily.

UC started receiving offers of help from universities around NZ and the world to take its students. UC chartered a plane to fly students over to Australia, with the University of Adelaide providing 167 students with tuition free of charge, and accommodation through their homestay programme or in a hall of residence.

A further 43 students went to the University of Oxford in England to study for a term. UC gave these students a special scholarship of $2,000 to cover international travel costs. The University of Oxford and its colleges waived tuition fees for all participants and also provided residential accommodation.

Within New Zealand, 67 students went on exchange to other New Zealand universities, with exchange agreements set up with the universities of Auckland, Auckland University of Technology (AUT), Massey, Victoria, Waikato and Otago. All of the universities involved in the exchange programme agreed not to charge fees for students.

The key feature of all these exchange arrangements was that the students remained enrolled as UC students. The generosity of this was remarkable. Many of the students had already paid their university enrolment fees and were locked into rental agreements for student flats or halls of residence in Christchurch. Allowing these students to remain enrolled as UC students meant that UC would not have to refund any much-needed enrolment income.

For the students, the exchanges presented a wonderful 'study abroad' experience. For the university, the programme helped UC's reputation for looking after their students, but more importantly, it gave it confidence that the students would return to UC once their exchange had finished.

The universities that came to the assistance of UC were '3am friends'. I first heard of the concept of 3am friends from Dave Parsons, who at the time was resilience manager for Sydney Water. He talks of 3am friends as those friends you feel you can call if you are in trouble – even if it is 3 o'clock in the morning. These friends will see your number flash up on their phone and they will take your call, even though they don't have to. Not only that, but these friends are willing to then get out of bed, in the middle of the night, to help you in any way they can.

As the Beatles song goes, 'We get by with a little help from our friends'. Few organizations have sufficient in-house resources to manage every eventuality. It would neither be efficient nor effective. A better strategy is to create a network of friends that your organization can call on for help in times of need. Friendships take work, though – they need to be nurtured proactively. This chapter provides ideas on how your organization can do this.

Imagine if you were to map out a network diagram that showed all of the people that you know that you could draw on for support in times of need. In most cases you would have several different clusters of connections, representing the different facets of your life – there will be family members, friends, workmates, people whom you know through various clubs or groups you belong to. Your connection to some of these people will be very strong (such as to family members or to close friends) and weaker for those whom you know less well, say for example a new work colleague.

If you then drew links between people within your network who knew each other, you would again find certain clusters. For example, it is likely that all your close friends will know and also be friends with each other. They are less likely, however, to know people that you are connected to through other spheres of your life. So, for example, your friends are far less likely to know all of your work colleagues (unless you regularly have parties that bring the two groups together). You can do the same thing for your organization – mapping out the network of 'friends' (be they individuals or organizations) that your organization could call on to assist in times of adversity.

When it comes to social networks there are different aspects that help in times of adversity.

Size

Network size is the number of people you are connected to. The more people you have good relationships with, the more sources of support you have to draw on in times of crisis. Quantity alone, however, is not the only aspect of your network of support to consider; it needs to be coupled with three other important characteristics.

Diversity

Diversity within your social network is also important. If you only connect with people with similar backgrounds and skills to your own, your exposure to different ideas and expertise is limited. When trouble strikes, if you can't solve the problem yourself, what you need is access to people with a different skill-set from yours. Knowing 20 plumbers isn't much help if what you really need to solve your problem is a window glazer. Of the plumbers that you know, though, many of them will have worked on building sites and will know a few glaziers.

Connectivity

Connectivity relates to your ability to leap beyond the immediate network of people that you know. There are some people in this world who have a very large and diverse network. These people are like hubs within a social network – they know nearly everybody. If you have a hub within your social network, this provides you with bridging capital into another world.[2] Connectors don't have to be well connected, though. The connector you need might just be someone who moves in different circles from you, and therefore knows people you don't. Sometimes the people we don't know well can be the best link into other social networks that we otherwise wouldn't be aware of.

Whether these connectors within your network are willing to grant you access to their network (ie using up some of their social capital in order to help you) depends on the fourth attribute you want in your network – quality.

Quality

Quality relates to the nature of the relationship you have with someone: how strong your relationship with them is, and the likelihood of their being willing to help you when you need it. Essentially, whether they are a 3am or a fair-weather friend! The quality of the relationship is an important aspect to consider.

Creating effective partnerships

Supply chains are an excellent example of organizational networks in action, and so are good places to start when considering how effectively your organization is developing and maintaining its relationships.

The resilience of your organization is critically dependent upon your suppliers and customers. Far too often, organizations select supply-chain partners based on a short-term view of getting the lowest price possible, without considering the ability of suppliers to deliver quality products or services during non-normal circumstances, or the willingness and capability of supply-chain partners to work constructively together to address complex challenges should they arise.

Creating resilient supply chains goes far beyond ensuring that you have the right contractual arrangements in place. It may be your supplier's fault and liability if it can't deliver to you – but it is still your problem when the supplies your organization needs aren't available.

There is a great little game that I had students play in a course I used to teach on systems thinking. The game was called the Beer Game[3] and it mimics a really simple supply chain where there is a manufacturer, a distributor and a retailer, all needing to keep their stocks of beer at the right levels. Hold too much stock of beer, and it costs them financially. Hold too little stock of beer, and they might not be able to supply their customers that week, which costs them even more in both lost sales and reputation.

The students are broken into three groups, representing the management teams of the manufacturer, distributer and retailer, and they have to decide in each round how many crates of beer they are going to order from their supplier (or produce in the case of the manufacturer). Each round represents a week, and there are time lags in the system. From the time the manufacturer decides to make beer, it takes two weeks before that beer becomes available to ship to the distributor. If the retailer orders 20 crates of beer this week, it doesn't get delivered to the shop until the following week. It is a classic systems problem, where each team is trying to optimize the supply-chain logistics from its own perspective, but because they are not coordinating with each other, disaster inevitably occurs. Usually the game degenerates into a series of boom/bust cycles until someone goes out of business.

There are several variants to the game, but what often happens is that the retailers are seeing customer orders come in at a relatively steady rate. The retail team focuses on honing its just-in-time style of ordering, minimizing its levels of inventory and maximizing profitability. The distributors follow suit, as do the manufacturers. The supply chain runs smoothly for the first few rounds, as just-in-time delivery works a charm. Then the weather warms up and customers have an increased thirst for beer.

The increased demand is a subtle change – not enough to raise the alarm for any of the teams, but slowly the retailers and distributors are increasing their weekly orders. The problem emerges from the delays in the system. It takes time to get the increased order communicated to the manufacturer, and for the extra supplies of beer to be made and shipped to the retailer.

The retailing team is getting worried. It placed a large order several weeks back, but it still hasn't seen any increased supply. Its inventory is running low and customer demand is still steadily increasing. The retailer feels it is time for drastic action – it puts in an even larger order to try to ensure it has security of supply.

The distributor's inventory has run out. It is only able to ship to the re-tailer what it receives from the manufacturer – and there is a large mismatch between what is being ordered and what is being delivered. It doesn't want to find itself in this position again, so it adds a large margin to its order, as a way of rebuilding its inventory.

Meanwhile the manufacturer is seeing an almost exponential increase in the sales of its product. It ramps up production significantly, and after a month or so, it seems to be finally getting on top of everything. Then, suddenly orders for its product completely dry up. The warm weather has passed and both the re-tailer and the distributer have suddenly found themselves holding more inven-tory than they can handle. There won't be any more beer orders for the next couple of months. The manufacturer now has a cash-flow problem – it can't sustain such a long period of no production and soon goes out of business.

What is so interesting about the Beer Game is that the same result hap-pens nearly every time. The players can see what is happening, but feel powerless to prevent the crash from occurring. There is nothing wrong with the intelligence or the intentions of the management teams – the dysfunction occurs because of the supply-chain system dynamics. We then talk with the students about how to redesign the supply-chain relationships so that there can be more resilient outcomes.

The Beer Game is a very simple representation of what can happen within a supply chain. It is easy to think that it could never occur in today's sophis-ticated world of supply-chain management. But, just a few years ago I had a friend working with a large office supplies company when its major com-petitor suffered a crisis with its distribution system. Rather than being a boon for her firm, the competitor's crisis spread disruption like a contagion right throughout the sector. News that one of the key suppliers was having trouble delivering made customers nervous. All of a sudden, rather than pur-chasing supplies on an as-needed basis, they suddenly started buying in bulk 'just in case'. For my friend's company, not only was it left trying to fill extra customer orders, but it was also seeing major pendulum swings in pur-chasing behaviour – with people buying in bulk one month, and then not buying at all the next. Its distribution systems were sent into chaos and it couldn't have been more relieved when its competitor resolved its problems and the market eventually stabilized.

Many of the problems highlighted within the Beer Game can be resolved with state-of-the-art supply-chain management techniques. Delays can be reduced. Transparency can be created within the supply chain so that people can see supply and demand projections. Diversity can be created across the supply chain so that there are no single points of failure. Something that cannot be easily re-engineered is the level of trust and willingness to co-operate between supply-chain partners.

During times of crisis, relationships come under pressure. The extent to which organizations are willing to work together, sometimes to their own short-term disadvantage, depends on the quality of the relationship that has been established over the previous months and years.

In the middle of the night, on Saturday, 3 August 2013, the global dairy giant Fonterra issued a statement to the media: 'Fonterra advises of quality issue'.[4] Fonterra had just advised eight of its wholesale customers that one of its products, a whey protein concentrate, potentially contained a micro-organism linked with botulism – a rare but life-threatening condition which can cause paralysis. Whey concentrate is used as an ingredient in a number of different products, including baby and infant milk formula.

The public reaction was one of immediate concern. Infant formula is one of those products that you just do not want any safety concerns over. Five years before, in China, six babies had died and an estimated 54,000 babies were hospitalized from formula that had been intentionally mixed with melamine – a chemical used in plastics manufacturing. With a customer base highly sensitized to infant formula safety concerns, Fonterra needed to handle the situation well.

Whey concentrate is sold to numerous different manufacturers around the world. As Fonterra scrambled to trace the affected product, it soon discovered that its systems were not set up to enable it to easily track where and when the batch in question had gone. This placed the safety of entire product lines in question, rather than just specific batches of product. As safety regulators around the world became concerned, several countries imposed bans on imports and sales of Fonterra products, and manufacturers started issuing immediate product recalls.

Word then began to emerge that Fonterra had known about the potential contamination for months, and the media storm began....

The contamination scare was traced back to an incident nearly 18 months earlier, when a torch broke during a maintenance inspection and a piece of plastic fell into a batch of whey powder. This batch was isolated and three months later the whey was 'reworked' to find the lost shard of plastic. The batch was re-wet and sieved to find the missing piece of plastic. The whey was then dried again back into powder form.

Re-wetting is not usually done within the whey plant and required some improvisation. Unfortunately, this improvisation involved using a stainless steel pipe, which hadn't been used for two years, and two pieces of flexible pipe. While these pipes were cleaned prior to use, twice, it is likely that somewhere on these pipes was a micro-organism waiting for the right conditions to flourish.

With the pieces of broken torch now removed from the whey product, the batch started to be distributed to many different manufacturers and into numerous food products.

Ten months later, in March 2013, came the first indication of a problem emerging. One of Fonterra's customers had a product test come back indicating growth of anaerobic spore-forming bacteria. The customer immediately investigated the source of this high reading, tracing it back to a single ingredient – the batch of whey that had been reworked by Fonterra back in May 2012.

There are many kinds of microbe that could have triggered the positive test, some harmless and others highly toxic. Within much of the dairy industry, there was a belief that botulism isn't an issue for whey protein concentrates, so it was assumed that the contamination was almost certainly a harmless form of microbe. Fonterra nevertheless did go on to get further testing done.

The botulism microbe is very difficult to test for reliably. The best method for detection is to give the product to a group of mice. If the mice survive, the product is probably safe. If any of the mice die, the product is potentially unsafe. As a test it has several drawbacks – not least because a mouse can die from unrelated causes.

One of the mice given the whey died, so botulism could not be ruled out. Fonterra convened its crisis response team, customers and regulators, the stock market was notified and the media release was sent out – at 12.32 am on a Saturday morning.

Although Fonterra, in theory, had many months of forewarning of potential issues with the batch of whey, in reality it was blindsided by the positive test result. And this showed. In the first few days it appeared to be slow in its crisis response, not knowing the answers to many vital questions. Which products were affected? Were there products still on supermarket shelves or being used in people's homes that might put their babies at risk?

One of the challenges adding confusion was that Fonterra had recently changed its IT system for managing the flow of its products. In an unlucky turn of events, the timing of that IT changeover had been at about the same time that the batch of affected whey had been sent out to customers. This meant it became quite a manual process to trace every last pallet containing the whey protein – which by now had been used as an ingredient in a myriad of other products.

Fonterra did its best to get information out quickly on which infant formulas were affected, but some of this information had to be later retracted because of inaccuracies. One of the products that had been recommended to parents for their babies turned out to be potentially contaminated. It took until 18 August – two weeks after the crisis broke – for Fonterra to be able to confirm that all affected product had been traced. During this time its reputation took a severe hit.

The Fonterra name was associated with botulism and contaminated infant food in headlines around the world. Its key customers were losing millions of dollars as consumers rapidly switched away from products that had been brought under a cloud of suspicion. Fonterra also faced strained relations with its regulator, whom it had failed to notify within 24 hours of becoming aware of a potential food safety issue. The reputational damage had knock-on ramifications for the entire New Zealand dairy sector. Frustrations were compounded by Fonterra's apparent self-centred attitude. A number of Fonterra's key stakeholders felt that the company had a 'Fortress Fonterra' mentality.

Frustrations between the New Zealand government and Fonterra became an undercurrent for how the crisis played out over the following weeks, to the extent that Ministry officials were sent to Fonterra premises to ensure that information the company supplied during the unfolding crisis was accurate.

On 28 August, 25 days after the crisis broke in world news, subsequent testing results revealed that the whey was not contaminated with botulism, but a similar type of microbe that is not toxigenic. In other words, the earlier testing had involved a 'false positive'. Consumers were never in danger.

The Fonterra case study illustrates two key points. The first is that understanding your organization's value chain matters. It is important for any organization to invest in the tools and technologies for facilitating these relationships so that they are not only efficient and effective during day-to-day operations, but are also fit for purpose during times of crisis.

This case study also provides a salient lesson in the need to monitor the *quality* of the relationships with your value-chain partners. Some of Fonterra's key stakeholders felt that the company had an overriding focus on its own immediate interests – sensing that the company wasn't really concerned about the interests of others, or its relationships with them. In the words of one of the inquiries conduced after the crisis: 'One of the most important steps Fonterra should now take is to use this opportunity to review both the substance and the style of its engagement with the people, organizations and communities that are important to it, to re-establish trust and to build lasting, mutually-beneficial relationships' (WPC Inquiry Committee, 2013, p 26 (4)).

Fonterra hadn't invested nearly enough time and effort into building itself a network of true 3am friends. In Fonterra's case, it was lucky and support was forthcoming. Fonterra is such a large player in the market that all those involved, including the New Zealand government, had a vested interest in helping it to resolve its problem. Had it been a smaller player in the market, it is quite conceivable that its 'Fortress Fonterra' attitude could have been its undoing.

Because no organization operates in isolation, there are inevitably risks that come from being connected to so many other organizations. In a world of globalization, where supply networks look more like 'supply webs' rather than 'supply chains', there are both positives and negatives that come from being interconnected to the fate of so many other organizations. One challenge is just how quickly and how far disruption can spread.

Resilience is a team sport – why your problem is my problem

There was a particularly wet rainy season in Thailand in 2011.[5] Tropical storm Haima hit in June, causing several of the country's free-flowing rivers to burst their banks and flood. From the end of July through to October, four more major storms hit the country. Rainfall in July and September was higher than any recorded during 1971 to 2000. Dams were full to capacity – there was simply too much water for the system to manage.

As flooding slowly moved towards the south, it inundated a series of industrial estates. Prior to 2011, none of the industrial parks in Thailand had flooded in the past 40 years. Seven were inundated during the month of October. Floodwaters reached Bangkok in late October, and the flood situation in the city remained grim until the end of November. The 2011 flooding in Thailand was assessed by the World Bank as the world's fourth-costliest disaster to date, and the world's worst flood disaster in terms of consequential losses.

Eight hundred companies, predominantly in the manufacturing sector, were located within the seven industrial parks that were inundated. The manufacturing industry makes up nearly 40 per cent of Thailand's GDP, so disruption to this sector had major ramifications. The problems created did not just have an impact on Thailand's economy – it sent ripples through global supply chains around the world, particularly in Japan. Thailand is one of the production hubs for global automobile manufacturers, and Japanese auto-makers were particularly hard hit. Of the 800 companies located in the affected industrial parks, 57 per cent were owned or operated by Japanese companies.

Toyota had three factories in the affected regions. Two-metre-high sandbag dykes guarded the entrance gates to Toyota's plants in Samut Prakarn and Chachoengsao province as the company prepared for the imminent floodwaters. Each factory was also ringed by a 1.2-metre flood wall, and a third set of flood barriers was placed inside each plant to protect machinery that couldn't be moved.

Its third plant, in Chachoengsao province, was more than 40 metres above sea level and therefore out of reach of the floodwaters.

Toyota's preparations served it well. None of its factories were flooded – but its operations ground to a halt all the same.

Starting from 10 October, Toyota had to suspend production at its Thai factories owing to supply shortages. Its suppliers were either submerged or inaccessible because of floodwaters. This was a serious blow for Toyota; Thailand is its third-largest production base outside Japan. Its operations in Thailand weren't able to resume until a long 42 days later.

The impact of the floods on Toyota was not isolated to Thailand, however – disruption quickly spread to other locations. Toyota had to cancel overtime at all its Japanese vehicle plants, causing a production loss of 7,000 vehicles a week. Not only that, but it also had to suspend production at plants in North America, Indonesia, Vietnam, the Philippines, Canada and South Africa because of a lack of critical parts from Thailand.

The Thailand floods highlight how the consequences of disruption can spread far beyond the geographic reach of any flood waters. The implication is that you can't just look internally to understand your organization's resilience – you also need to consider the broader system within which your organization is operating. How resilient is your local community? How resilient is your industry sector? The resilience of these larger contexts will influence both the frequency and severity of disruptions your organization is likely to face.

As part of any resilience-building programme, therefore, it is important to reach out and invite others to join you on your journey to become more resilient. This not only offers moral support for the inevitable bumps in the road that your organization may face as it develops its resilience, but also provides a much stronger network of friends on whom you can rely when trouble strikes.

So far in this chapter I have been talking about relationships between organizations. But the dynamics of those relationships really come down to people and how well they connect with each other. There is nothing like knowing the person at the end of the phone when you have to call at 3 am to ask for help. Also, help, when you need it, doesn't always come from an organization that you have dealt with previously – it can emerge from unexpected quarters. Your people have their own personal social capital, which, if they are so inclined, they can tap to support your organization.

Building social capital

After the first Christchurch earthquake, I was contacted by Dave Parsons from Sydney Water, wanting to know how we were all doing. He was also curious to see how the water infrastructure in Christchurch was holding up, so I put him in touch with Onno Mulder. Onno is the CEO of City Care, the city's major contractor that maintains the city's water and wastewater networks. An invitation was extended to Onno, whenever he felt ready, to give a presentation on his experience to a group of Australian water utilities. It was an offer that Onno took up a few months later.

This serendipitous connection reaped benefits for Christchurch when, just a few months after that presentation, the city was struck by an even more devastating earthquake. With a deeper understanding of what the Christchurch water and wastewater repair teams would be facing, support rallied from around Australia to provide Christchurch with practical support in getting its sewage and water systems repaired. This help was more than just lip service; a taskforce of 12 sucker trucks and their specialist crews were sent to New Zealand to help clear pipes of the silt and mud that had boiled up during the earthquake.

For the Australian water companies, this was a chance for them to test how their mutual aid agreements worked in the first-ever global deployment of its kind. It also provided their crews with valuable experience of working in a post-disaster environment. For Christchurch, this help was invaluable and hugely appreciated, and it all came about through an opportune connection.

Joanne Stevenson[6] spent her PhD exploring how organizations throughout Canterbury drew on their social capital, following the earthquakes, to support their recovery. Coining the concept of 'relational resilience', Jo's study confirmed that resilience can be created through patterns of interaction between organizations and people. She found that organizations with the ability to form and manage their networks effectively were better able to access the right kinds of support when they needed it. They were also better at maintaining positive relationships with those they might need or want to work with in the future.

One of the things that I found fascinating about Jo's work was the different ways that organizations structured their support interactions (Figure 4.1). Jo's research found that it is not enough to have a network of supporters; your organization must also have the capacity to locate, activate and apply the benefits of these external sources of resilience. The most notable difference between organizations that effectively mobilized relational resilience and those that did not was whether they managed their network as a collective resource rather than as a series of individual interactions.

Figure 4.1 Examples of different support network structures used by organizations during crisis recovery

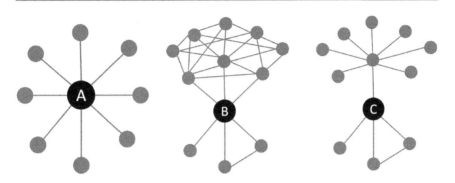

Jo found that organizations with relatively unconnected networks (such as Organization A in Figure 4.1) were on average less successful at recovering from the earthquakes. Organizations with unconnected networks tended to rely on arm's-length, formal, or market ties with their supporters. Tending to view the support as a transactional relationship, they demonstrated relatively low levels of reciprocity (where support is offered in both directions). They also tended to have little involvement with business associations or other groups that have important bridging and bonding roles to access resources from further afield. Ultimately this hampered their recovery.

The other two types of support network structure in Figure 4.1 have much greater levels of connectivity within their networks, but in different ways. Organization B's network is characterized by the formation of a group of supporters, working together for mutual benefit. This clique of organizations found ways to reduce the time and effort required to keep everyone informed by forming an unofficial group. This way, instead of having repeat conversations with others in similar situations, they communicated with the clique en masse, not only reducing the total number of phone calls, meetings and e-mails needed but also increasing the total amount of information exchanged. Organization C utilizes a coordinator – informally assigning a particularly well-connected network member the role of 'support coordinator' as a way of reducing the burden of distributing and taking in support. Both of these strategies served to reduce the time and energy required by the organization to maintain its network. The organization had fewer one-on-one engagements to manage but still benefited from a large number of supporters.

Of even greater importance than the shape of an organization's network, however, was the nature of the relationships that organizations had with their supporters. In Jo's study she found that the help and advice that businesses found to be most valuable came from those people with whom they already had an established and trusted relationship. At times, even if the new relationship had more expertise (such as legal or accounting advice), people tended to value (and follow) the advice of close family and friends and trusted colleagues much more.

Organizations therefore need to invest in developing sustained, trust-based relationships with a diverse set of other organizations to support their resilience. In a world of budget cutbacks, this can seem like a daunting prospect, but as the following case study demonstrates, it can be done – you just need to think creatively about the ways to achieve it.

Over 45,000 children are reported missing in Canada each year. There is a saying that it takes a whole village to raise a child. The corollary is that it takes a community to find a child. The more eyes on the lookout, the greater the chances of quickly locating a missing child and safely reuniting them with their family. To this end, an exciting partnership has emerged between the Missing Children Society of Canada (MSCS), corporate partners and law enforcement agencies, combining technology with philanthropy to deliver CodeSearch.[7]

CodeSearch is an app that sends out targeted alerts to people who are in the local area where a child has gone missing or is expected to be located. Not everyone watches or listens to the news, so by delivering real-time alerts and information, CodeSearch is a way to activate a search capability rapidly, taking away vital time for an abductor to make an escape.

The involvement of corporations in CodeSearch, however, is what makes this initiative so interesting. CodeSearch essentially turns employees into field agents, who can be eyes and ears on the ground when a child goes missing in their local area. Along with notifications, CodeSearch participants also provide local expertise and resources.

To illustrate the power of this kind of network, one of the founding corporate partners for the project is Westjet. Westjet is a low-cost airline that flies throughout Canada. Westjet is such an important partner in the CodeSearch initiative because one of the first places an abductor will often go is to the airport. With their 10,000 employees ready to receive an alert if a child goes missing in their local area, employees are engaged in the first-ever rapid response network for missing children.

WestJet helps MSCS search for missing children by providing free flights to the charity's investigators, who travel all over Canada and internationally to find children. WestJet also works with the society to provide the logistics behind reuniting missing children with their families.

Organizations often want to improve the communities they serve. From a resilience perspective, corporate social responsibility programmes can also be designed to help build social capital. The sort of partnership that Westjet has developed with the MCSC enables it to contribute to its community in a way that resonates with their employees. By empowering its employees to become active participants in the programme, it is not only helping to find missing kids, but is also building strong social capital. Its people work alongside others from many different organizations, all with the common goal of finding missing kids. That is a cache of trusted relationships, knowledge and intelligence that any organization would love to have when crisis strikes.

Summary

Here are some key take-outs from this chapter:

- The way your organization operates during the day-to-day influences the extent to which people and organizations will be prepared to help you during times of adversity – be a 3am friend to others and they are more likely to be a 3am friend to you.

- Look beyond your organization to see the resilience of the broader system within which you operate – help other organizations to become more resilient, as their resilience impacts yours.

- To manage change and adversity successfully requires support from many different quarters – invest in developing and sustaining trust-based relationships with a broad network of organizations.

Quick Start Guide: Leveraging your social capital during a crisis

The relationships your organization has fostered over time are a significant asset during times of crises – be sure to utilize them:

Reach out. During a crisis, many of us become defensive and withdraw from people, but this is the worst possible response for your business. People cannot help you if they do not understand your situation. Although you might think everyone knows what is going on, they may not. Be the one to reach out – make the phone-call.

Give in order to receive.	If you want people to help you during times of crisis, you need to be prepared to help others when they are in crisis. This karma will often come back to you in unexpected ways.
Be nice.	People don't have to help you – they need to want to help you. And yet, when we are stressed and under pressure, we are often abrupt and abrasive. Always try to find ways to nurture the relationship.
Be specific about the help you need.	Many people might want to help, but they don't know how. Sit down and make a wish-list of those things you would really like right now – it might be a confidant to bounce ideas off, someone to pick up your kids from school, temporary premises to work from or specialist advice. Get your needs clear in your mind, so that when people offer, you can suggest the best ways for them to help.
Try to be open.	Help will often come from unexpected quarters, so talk to many different people and try to be open about the situation. If people feel that your situation is highly confidential, they can't reach into their networks to find the help you need.
Keep checking in.	Crises often move rapidly. What you need today is not likely to be what you need next week. Keep people updated with the latest situation so that the ways they help you can evolve in sync.

Resilience initiatives – building effective partnerships

At the end of this book are a number of different initiatives that organizations can to use to improve their resilience. The initiatives with particular relevance for building effective partnerships are:

1   Get someone in to tell their story.

3   Use a little peer pressure.

9   Partner with other organizations to benchmark and improve resilience together.

24 Establish mutual aid agreements.

25 Make resilience a core focus of procurement.

26 Organize social events with partners.

27 Help someone out.

28 Take the time to get to know people.

35 Draw in fresh perspectives.

48 Run exercises with other organizations.

49 Socialize your plans.

53 Make sure you can contact people.

54 Prepare key communications messages in advance.

59 Focus on knowledge transfer gaps.

60 Encourage cross-department working.

References and further reading

A good way to find copies of academic papers is via Google Scholar: https://scholar.google.com

1   Two books that provide further insights into the University of Canterbury's emergency preparedness and what helped them to recover from the Canterbury earthquakes are:

–   Seville, E, Hawker, C and Lyttle, J (2012) *Resilience Tested: A year and a half of 10,000 aftershocks*, University of Canterbury, http://www.canterbury.ac.nz/emergency/documents/resiliencetested.pdf

–   Seville, E, Hawker, C and Lyttle J (2011) *Shaken but not Stirred: A university's resilience in the face of adversity*, University of Canterbury, http://www.canterbury.ac.nz/emergency/documents/shakenbutnotstirred.pdf

2   Social networks

–   Aldrich, DP (2012) *Building Resilience: Social capital in post-disaster recovery*, University of Chicago Press, Chicago

–   Barabasi, AL (2002) *Linked: How everything is connected to everything else and what it means*, Plume, New York

3 The Beer Game is a role-play simulation game that lets players experience typical coordination problems of (traditional) supply chains, in which information sharing and collaboration do not exist. In more general terms, this supply chain represents any non-coordinated system in which problems arise due to lack of systemic thinking. For more details, see: http://www.beergame.org/

4 Fonterra botulism scare:

- WPC80 Inquiry Committee (2013) *Report of Independent Inquiry for Fonterra Board*, 23 October, http://wpc80-inde-report.fonterra.com/media/280378/wpc80-inquiry-full-report.pdf

- Government Inquiry into the Whey Protein Concentrate Contamination Incident (2014) *The WPC80 incident: causes and responses*, http://www.dia.govt.nz/vwluResources/Government-Whey-Inquiry-Report-November-2014/$file/Government-Whey-Inquiry-Report-November-2014.PDF

- International Commission on Microbiological Specifications for Foods (2013) *Usefulness of testing for Clostridium botulinum in powdered infant formula and dairy-based ingredients for infant formula*, http://www.icmsf.org/pdf/icmsf_infant_formula_testing_27_aug_2013.pdf

- Henson, N (2015) Government distrust of Fonterra 'staggering', *Waikato Times*, 11 February, http://www.stuff.co.nz/business/farming/dairy/66067708/Government-distrust-of-Fonterra-staggering

5 Thailand flooding the automotive industry

- The World Bank (2012) *Thai Flood 2011: Rapid assessment for resilient recovery and reconstruction planning*, The World Bank, http://documents.worldbank.org/curated/en/2012/01/16360869/thai-flood-2011-rapid-assessment-resilient-recovery-reconstruction-planning-vol-1-2-overview

- ADPC (2014) *Towards a Resilient Business Community in Thailand: Small and medium sized enterprises (SMEs) and disaster risk reduction (DRR)*, Asian Disaster Preparedness Centre, http://www.adpc.net/igo/category/ID782/doc/2015-vAqd7G-ADPC-SME_Report_Final13_Jan.pdf

- Mukai, A, Hagiwara, Y and Horie, M (2011) Thai floods disrupting Japanese car production worldwide: cars, *Bloomberg*, 31 October, http://www.bloomberg.com/news/articles/2011-10-31/thai-floods-disrupting-japanese-car-production-worldwide-cars

- Haraguchi, M and Lall, U (2015) Flood risks and impacts: a case study of Thailand's floods in 2011 and research questions for supply chain decision making, *International Journal of Disaster Risk Reduction*, **14**, pp 256–72, http://water.columbia.edu/files/2014/10/supply_chain_Thailand.pdf

- Toyota (2012) *Toyota Annual Report 2012*, Toyota, http://www.toyota-global.com/investors/ir_library/annual/pdf/2012/

- Guy Carpenter (2012) *Thailand Floods 2011: One year retrospective*, Guy Carpenter, http://www.guycarp.com/content/dam/guycarp/en/documents/

dynamic-content/Thailand%20Flood%202011_One%20Year%20
Retrospective.pdf

6 Joanne Stevenson is a Senior Research Consultant with Resilient Organisations. Jo started her PhD soon after the first of Christchurch's earthquakes. As a social geographer, she was interested in the embeddedness of organizations within a community, and the networks of support that these organizations drew on to facilitate their recovery. It was a fascinating piece of research.

– Stevenson, JR (2014) *Organisational Resilience After the Canterbury Earthquakes: A contextual approach*, PhD Thesis, University of Canterbury, http://www.resorgs.org.nz/images/stories/pdfs/Organizationsfacingcrisis/ stevensonjr_phdthesis_v3.pdf

7 CodeSearch and Westjet:

– Missing Children Society of Canada (2016) *CodeSearch: A rapid response programme*, Missing Children Society of Canada website: http://mcsc.ca/ search-program/codesearch/

– Missing Children Society of Canada (2012) *CodeSearch*, YouTube video, https://www.youtube.com/watch?v=cGg94IuoCzA&feature=youtu.be

– Westjet (nd) *Community Investment: Missing Children Society of Canada*, http://www.westjet.com/guest/en/about/community-investment/missing- children.shtml

– Guillemaud, L (2013) *Join the world's largest online search party for missing children*, Westjet Blog, 16 July, http://blog.westjet.com/join-largest-online-search- party-missing-children/

– Gerstel, J (2011) These truly are the friendly skies, *Toronto Star*, 23 November, http://www.thestar.com/business/best_employers/2011/11/23/these_truly_are_ the_friendly_skies.html

– WestJet (2015) WestJet once again named one of Canada's 10 Most Admired Corporate Cultures for 2015, *Canada Newswire*, 20 November

Situation awareness – keeping a finger on the pulse

05

It was early in 2010 that inspectors from the International Atomic Energy Agency noticed something strange going on at the Natanz uranium enrichment plant in Iran.[1] Centrifuges, used to enrich uranium gas, were starting to fail at an unprecedented rate. What was causing the centrifuges to fail so regularly was a complete mystery – to the Iranians and international inspectors alike.

A few months later, a seemingly unrelated event occurred. A computer security firm was called in to troubleshoot a series of computers in Iran that were crashing and rebooting repeatedly. There, they discovered the world's first digital weapon – Stuxnet.

Stuxnet wasn't just any kind of computer virus. It was a worm, capable of spreading on its own over a computer network. Rather than simply hijacking targeted computers or stealing information from them, for the first time it demonstrated that a computer virus could wreak destruction in the physical world.

Stuxnet targeted a particular kind of computer system – SCADA. SCADA systems are used to monitor and control physical equipment remotely – gathering and analysing data in real time about how a system is operating. If a fault is detected, it will automatically raise the alarm or adjust settings as needed. SCADA are widely used in industry, helping to run power plants, oil and gas pipelines, water and wastewater treatment plants, and even metal detectors at airports.

Though Stuxnet had been discovered, the computer security experts still didn't really know what it did or at whom it was targeted. That took months of detective work to decipher. The computer security firm set about identifying 'markers' to locate infected computers. When looking at how far the worm had spread, a strange pattern emerged. Out of the initial 38,000 infections, about 22,000 were in Iran. These infection numbers were way out of sync with previous patterns of worldwide computer infections. Iran was usually never placed high, if at all, in infection statistics.

Initially the computer security experts thought that the worm may have spread predominantly in Iran owing to out-of-date security software. But then they realized that although the authors of the worm were ruthlessly intent on spreading their malware, it was in a strangely limited way. Unlike most malware, which used e-mail or malicious websites to infect masses of victims at once, none of Stuxnet's exploits leveraged the internet. Stuxnet could spread stealthily between computers – even those not connected to the internet.

They soon discovered that Stuxnet was spreading from one facility to another via USB drives. If a USB thumb drive was put into an infected machine, Stuxnet would worm its way onto it, then spread onto the next machine that read that USB drive. It appeared that the attackers were targeting systems they knew were not connected to the internet.

Delving deeper, computer security experts slowly narrowed the field of potential targets. Embedded in Stuxnet's code was a dossier detailing the specific technical configuration of the facility it sought. As soon as the worm arrived at a new network, it would wake up and ask four questions:

1   Am I in a network that's running a SCADA software control system?

2   Is the plant control made by a certain manufacturer?

3   Is it running a particular type of software?

4   Is this software contacting an electrical motor made by one of two companies?

If the answer to all four questions was yes, the worm must finally have found its way to its target. Any system that didn't match this configuration precisely would go unharmed – Stuxnet would shut itself down and move on to the next system until it found its victim. The only facility in Iran that met those four criteria was the Natanz uranium enrichment plant.

Everything about this worm was designed to help it remain undetected. Once Stuxnet reached the Natanz SCADA system, it sat quietly for two weeks before launching its attack. Then, rather than causing a catastrophic failure in the equipment, which might have led to investigation, the worm just made subtle changes. First, it slowly increased the frequency on spinning centrifuges for 15 minutes, before restoring them to normal. In the control room, everything appeared normal, as the worm replayed earlier recordings of the plant's protection system values during the attack. The worm then waited 27 days before making its next move – this time reducing the frequency on the centrifuges. The worm then waited another 27 days before repeating the same sequence. The extreme range of frequencies slowly but surely destroyed the life of the uranium enrichment centrifuges.

The creators of Stuxnet have never been officially identified. The size and sophistication of the worm, however, led experts to believe that it could have been created only with the sponsorship of a nation-state – with strong suspicions it was the United States or Israel.

Although Stuxnet's stealth attack has now been uncovered, its potential powers of destruction have not necessarily been curtailed. The Stuxnet worm infected millions of computers around the world – but because they are not the defined target, it remains inactive. The proliferation of the worm, however, means that it is now in the hands of many people – with the potential that it will be reverse engineered and morphed for new purposes.

The Stuxnet attack has also provided a useful blueprint to future attackers by highlighting the route to infiltrate hard targets – contractors. Pretty much every industrial or military facility around the world uses contractors. A few USB sticks dropped in the facility carpark, waiting to be picked up and unsuspectingly plugged into a computer, can be all it takes to unleash havoc.

It is hard to know if or how many such attacks have actually taken place. In 2009, oil, gas and petrochemical companies such as Exxon, Shell and BP, among others, were hit by the Night Dragon virus, which was distributed using spear phishing. The virus allowed the infected computers to be controlled remotely by attackers. There was no physical damage caused, but the attackers were able to access operational blueprints for SCADA systems and collected data.

Then, in 2014, Germany's Federal Office for Information Security (or BSI) reported a digital attack on a steel mill. Although details regarding the incident are vague, the report stated that malware was used to cause the breakdown of individual control components. The attackers used spear-phishing e-mails and sophisticated social engineering to gain access to the steel mill's office network, leading them to the production network. The attackers then caused the uncontrolled shutdown of a blast furnace, resulting in massive damage.

US Defense Secretary Leon Panetta has warned that the United States is vulnerable to a cyber-Pearl Harbor. An aggressor nation or extremist group could use cyber tools to gain control of critical switches – derailing trains, contaminating water supplies or shutting down power grids across the country. The era of cyber attackers reaching into the physical world to create damage may have begun.

If cyber security isn't already a major area of concern for your organization, it probably will be soon. In the words of the Director of the FBI: 'I am convinced that there are only two types of companies: those that have been hacked and those that will be. And even they are converging into one category: companies that have been hacked and will be hacked again.' (Mueller, 2012)

Cyber security is just one of many emerging threats facing organizations around the world. To be resilient, your organization needs good situation awareness so that it can spot sources of trouble on the horizon.

Situation awareness is a term that originally comes from the military. It refers to an ability to make sense of the current situation, how things are changing, and what that might mean for the future. Imagine you are a fighter pilot in a dog-fight. To survive, you not only have to understand where your plane currently is (ie how close you are to that nearby mountain range), you also have to understand your direction and speed of travel to be able to foresee where you are likely to be in a few seconds' time. Being in a dog-fight, though, it isn't only your plane that you need to think about. You also need to know where the other plane is and where it is also likely to be in a few seconds' time. This ability not only to sense the current situation, but also to project that forward in time and to understand its implications, makes the difference between those who survive the dog-fight and those who don't.

Building situation awareness

In late 2002, rumours of vinegar sales surging started emerging from southern China.[2] For members of the international public health community, this is the kind of early warning signal they look out for. Vinegar is commonly used in China as a disinfectant. If there is a run on vinegar, it is a sure sign that the population believe there is some kind of infectious disease on the rise.

In China, months before any official notification of an outbreak, rumours spread of a contagious illness in the Guangdong Province. Believing that fumigating a room with boiling vinegar could prevent illness from spreading, people rushed out to buy vinegar and panic buying began. Some shops ran out of vinegar and in other places prices skyrocketed. Severe acute respiratory syndrome – which we now know as SARS – was spreading.

The World Health Organization (WHO) has only a short window of time to stamp out an impending contagious disease outbreak before it spreads exponentially. It therefore needs a head start on identifying and investigating emerging outbreaks. With some authorities reluctant to report an outbreak, formal notification is not always forthcoming. The WHO therefore has to think of other ways to build its situation awareness. Between 1997 and 2000, the WHO helped to establish the Global Outbreak Alert and Response Network (GOARN). The GOARN network has over 120 partners throughout the world and has responded to more than 50 outbreaks since it was formed. SARS was the first time that GOARN identified and responded to an outbreak that was rapidly spreading internationally.

GOARN is a collaboration of existing institutions and networks, constantly alert and ready to respond. Drawing on this network to scan the horizon and share information is a way for the international public health community to build its situation awareness to discover if something is amiss. This network has developed a number of tools to provide early warning. For example, the Global Public Health Intelligence Network (GPHIN), based in Canada, continuously searches the internet for news stories that might signal an impending public health concern. This sort of tool is important, as more than 60 per cent of initial outbreak reports tend to come from unofficial or informal sources.

The first clue regarding the SARS outbreak was detected on 27 November 2002 – just 11 days after the first reported case. GPHIN picked up reports of a 'flu outbreak' in China and forwarded them to the WHO. Unfortunately, no system is perfect. At the time, GPHIN wasn't set up for automatic translation. The Chinese news article wasn't translated into English until 21 January 2003. In the meantime, other rumours of a problem in China started to emerge. Despite repeated queries from the WHO to Chinese officials, further information was not forthcoming.

On 10 February 2003, nearly three months after the first known case, finally came information that sparked the global health response. The WHO office in Beijing received an e-mail describing a strange contagious disease that had already left more than 100 people dead in Guangdong Province in just one week. The e-mail described a panic attitude, with people emptying pharmaceutical stocks of any medicine they thought might protect them. Querying this with the Chinese authorities, the following day the WHO received a report acknowledging the unexplained pneumonia outbreak, reporting 300 cases of acute respiratory syndrome, with five deaths in Guangdong Province.

Over the next month, SARS travelled to Hong Kong, by way of an ill Chinese physician attending a wedding. In one night at a Hong Kong hotel, it spread from that man to at least 12 other people. These 12 returned to their five home countries and created multiple chains of transmission. Over the course of the next four months, SARS spread to every continent of the world, with more than 8,000 cases of SARS, resulting in almost 800 deaths in 27 countries.

As the international public health community rallied to halt the spread of SARS, the GOARN network proved pivotal. International experts and front-line clinicians came together via teleconferences, often daily, to share information, experiences and data in real time. There were also specialist groups that met to address particular themes. A clinicians' network was formed in order to find the best ways to treat the disease most effectively. Epidemiologists from around the world came together to examine how the disease was spreading and to determine the best containment strategies. There was also a laboratory network, focused on finding ways to characterize the agent(s) causing the illness and develop diagnostic tests.

During the outbreak, GOARN provided a framework for bringing together people with the right technical expertise from all around the world; for sharing information, data and experiences in real time; and for the collective discussion and evaluation of that information in very practical terms – so that it could be acted on at a local level. It was an impressive global response. The WHO declared SARS contained on 9 July 2003.

When a crisis is emerging, you might not get any warning bells flashing. To build your organization's situation awareness, you need to find ways to turn your people into sentinels – always on the lookout for signals of change. You also need to create mechanisms for gathering together all of that intelligence so that it can be understood in context.

Accurate prediction of the future isn't realistic. But your organization can arm itself with awareness of the possible futures that it may face. In a rapidly evolving threat environment, there are strategies you can use to improve your organization's situation awareness.

While your organization may not have the ability to create a tool as sophisticated as GOARN for scanning the horizon for emerging threats, you can tap into the underlying principle of the network – that someone, somewhere, will have seen the signals that a threat may be emerging. But because people are seeing these signals in isolation, they don't always have the context to recognize the potential threat or opportunity they represent. You need to find ways to encourage them to share this information.

There are many different ways you could encourage this – ranging from a simple 'suggestions box' through to dedicated horizon-scanning sessions with your team (for more ideas on this, see the initiatives chapter at the end of the book). What you want to create is a culture whereby anyone, from any level of your organization, feels both empowered and encouraged to speak up if they see something they think needs attention.

It does take significant courage for people to raise issues they foresee, particularly if their ideas diverge from the mainstream thinking within your organization. Think about that e-mail the WHO received on 10 February about people dying in Guangdong. The outbreak had been going on for several months at that point. What had prevented the sender from acting sooner? What may have triggered them to finally act? As you reflect on these questions, think about whether and under what situations people in your organization would be prepared to flag potential issues.

In the aviation industry (as well as many others), significant effort has been invested towards creating a culture where people come forward with information on safety issues, near-misses and actual incidents. Over the decades, researchers have identified common requirements for creating a reporting system that works:[3]

1 Provide ways for people to report confidentially or anonymously if they want to.

2 Have a separate team collecting and analysing the reports, one that is different from those with the authority to institute disciplinary proceedings and impose sanctions.

3 Provide rapid, useful, accessible and intelligible feedback on how the information has been acted on.

4 Don't make people fill in screeds of paperwork – make it as easy as possible to report something.

To really build a culture of constant horizon-scanning, however, I wouldn't just rely on a reporting system – it needs to be a more social process than that. Create forums within your organization for actively scanning the horizon for threats and opportunities. Team up with other organizations to collectively identify emerging trends. Have regular presentation sessions where a team member takes an emerging issue or trend and talks about the potential implications of this issue or trend for your organization. The idea is not to expect people to be able to forecast what will or won't occur, but to develop a mindset and the capability to explore alternative futures.

Once you have good practices in place for ensuring that your people are active sensors, on the lookout for and ready to share the information they collect, you then face your next challenge – what to do with all that information. Too much information can come across simply as noise. We therefore need to create strategies for reflecting on the signals being gathered.

There are an infinite number of events or changes going on in the world that could have implications for your organization. It might be the most inconspicuous set of circumstances that, together, can create the perfect storm. In the study of disasters, there is a well-known framework called the Swiss Cheese Model,[4] which highlights that it is rarely just one thing going wrong that leads to a major disaster. Disasters occur when an unfortunate set of circumstances converge. This requires a delicate balance to be struck in terms of situation awareness. You don't want to fall into the trap of reacting like a shadow boxer to every imagined potentiality; neither do you want to be caught unawares by an event because you weren't paying attention to the warning signals you were receiving.

Many organizations address this challenge by designing a suite of criteria for when and how employees should escalate issues upwards in their organization. These escalation procedures help ensure that senior managers are quickly alerted when conditions cross a predefined threshold. This process works well for events that are relatively familiar for the organization, and is definitely a best practice that I would recommend. The very process of thinking about what situations might signal an impending threat or crisis, and getting agreement within your organization of the thresholds for when the organization should react, is beneficial.

Escalation criteria, though, are less effective for situations where crises don't follow a well-defined pattern, or where a small trigger event initiates a cascade of events creating disproportionate effects. You can think about the development of a crisis a bit like a balloon.[5] Over time, within your organization's operating environment, there might be changes in small latent conditions that make your organization more crisis-prone. Essentially, each of these latent conditions puts a bit of extra air into the balloon. It might be something like an unusually high turnover of staff within a department, a new IT system being installed, the slow degradation of safety culture within your workplace, the global financial crisis putting your key customers under pressure, or a new competitor entering your market. On their own, any one of these situations is quite manageable. However, if you get too many of these latent conditions occurring simultaneously, it is a bit like putting too much air into a balloon. Once that balloon is highly pressurized, it takes just a minor touch with a pin to cause it to explode. If the balloon wasn't so full of air, the pin still would still cause damage, but the failure would be more of a slow deflation rather than a catastrophic explosion.

From a situation awareness perspective, it can be tempting to look out for the 'pin' to try to spot and prevent a trigger event from occurring. The pin, however, may emerge with little warning. A more fruitful endeavour is to monitor the amount of air in the balloon – constantly monitoring and addressing the status of latent conditions that will make your organization more crisis-prone.

Once you have all of the pieces of the puzzle, insight is still needed to imagine how a situation might potentially unfold. The skill of projection – being able to take your understanding of the current situation and its dynamics, and from that to evaluate what the implications are for the system at a future point in time – is most definitely an art rather than a science. None of us have a perfect crystal ball for predicting what the future may hold.

Sensing when to act

Forty years ago, public health officials held their breath to see if the world was about to experience another global pandemic.[6] In February 1976, an 18-year-old army private, David Lewis, was feeling achy and feverish. His head hurt, his nose was running, and he was shivering with cold. He was sent back to bed. That evening, though, he dragged himself out of bed, determined to complete a five-mile hike with his unit. Private Lewis never made it to the end of that hike – as he walked, he started to feel worse and worse. He couldn't get enough air into his lungs. Eventually Private Lewis collapsed. Though he was revived by his sergeant and immediately rushed to hospital, a few days later Private Lewis was dead.

Private Lewis wasn't the only soldier with flu-like symptoms. Flu had been circulating around the base for the past month. Most of the soldiers were suffering a common strand of flu, but a small number had a variety of flu that was unknown. Further testing revealed that the virus was H1N1 – commonly known as swine flu.

None of the soldiers had been in contact with pigs and, worryingly, there were similarities between this virus and the one that had swept around the world in 1918, killing more than 40 million people. Public health officials were understandably concerned. Was this the first sign of an impending pandemic, or just a random event that would fizzle into nothing?

In addition to Private Lewis, 13 other soldiers came down with the H1N1 strain of flu. Five hundred other soldiers tested positive for antibodies for the flu, clearly demonstrating human transmission. Winter then moved into spring. As the weather warmed up, the number of cases petered out.

What did this mean? Did the virus not have the capability to spread easily, or was it just the calm before the storm? Would the next winter see the virus spread like wildfire? The question facing public health officials was this: should they attempt a pre-emptive strike by vaccinating people to prevent a recurrence of the 1918 pandemic?

In the pandemic years of 1957 and 1968, each time the pandemics had peaked before sufficient vaccine could be distributed. Could early detection this time be a unique opportunity to get ahead of the virus and to vaccinate before it spread too far? It was a tantalizing prospect.

But to undertake a successful vaccination programme was not going to be easy. There were significant logistical issues to overcome. The pharmaceutical industry had just finished manufacturing the flu vaccine to be used for the coming year. Vaccine is produced in fertilized eggs, and the roosters used for this process were about to be culled. If they were, the industry could not resume production for several months. Even with the roosters available, vaccine production is not a quick process. They would need to start immediately if they wanted enough vaccine to beat the coming flu season.

The decision to act was made. In late March, President Ford announced the government's plan to vaccinate every man, woman and child in the United States. The 1976 swine flu vaccination programme was under way.

During the five-month interval while the new vaccine was being prepared, no additional cases of influenza from this swine virus were reported. This caused some in the scientific community to pause and question the wisdom of proceeding. Others, however, felt that the risks associated with waiting were too great. Mass immunization of the US population began in October 1976. The vaccination programme immunized 45 million people in 10 weeks.

Coupled with the vaccination, an intensive programme of surveillance and monitoring was also implemented. As the winter season approached, there were no cases of swine influenza detected until 19 November, when a single case was detected in Missouri. After that, no more cases were reported.

In November, a patient in Minnesota who had received the vaccine came down with Guillain–Barré Syndrome (GBS). GBS is particularly nasty autoimmune disease that can be triggered by a range of things, including flu. The first symptoms are numbness, tingling and pain. This is then followed by weakness of the legs and arms that progressively creeps up the body over time. In a quarter of all patients, GBS can affect their breathing muscles – without a ventilator they would die. Even with appropriate care, GBS is fatal in 5 per cent of cases. As GBS takes hold, the weakness gets progressively worse. This can continue for anywhere between half a day to a month, before the patient plateaus and finally begins the journey to improvement.

In December, additional cases of GBS were reported in Minnesota and Alabama. During the following month, over 50 cases of GBS from 11 states were reported from people who had recently received the vaccine. It is now estimated that in the six weeks after receiving their swine flu vaccination, people's chances of contracting GBS increased to 1 in 100,000 – a nearly 10-fold increase in risk. There are multiple theories on why this particular vaccination programme led to increased risk, but the exact reason still remains unknown today.

Although the chances of any individual getting GBS following vaccination were very small, because of the sheer number of people being vaccinated it is estimated that somewhere in the vicinity of 500 people potentially contracted GBS as a direct result of the 1976 vaccination programme. On 16 December 1976, with concerns about the side effects rising, the national vaccine campaign was terminated.

The 1976 swine flu serves as a cautionary tale. Now, with the benefit of hindsight, we know that the decision to vaccinate in 1976 wasn't the right one. But 40 years later, if people were making a decision based on the same information they had available to them at the time, would a different decision be made? To roll out a vaccination campaign effectively, with the technology and distribution logistics of the time, required choices to be made with imperfect knowledge. No option was risk-free. Delay immunization for too long, waiting for spread to be confirmed, and the disease might spread faster than your ability to vaccinate. Today, despite modern advances in microbiology, health officials still make decisions in a cloud of uncertainty.

The 1976 swine flu vaccination programme illustrates the challenges in deciding how to respond to emerging threats. Respond too quickly and you may respond unnecessarily as the threat proves to be ultimately insignificant; wait too long and the threat may grow and you have missed the opportunity to mount an effective response.

Crises are characterized by uncertainty and speed. The situation may be evolving rapidly and yet we feel pressure to be seen as 'decisive'. To address these competing forces, I suggest mapping out a decision timeline, with clear decision points for when key choices need to be made. Buy yourself time by staging your decisions.

Staged decision making is a way of being decisive where you need to be, while leaving yourself with real options and future choices where you can. In the 1976 swine flu example, the decision to proceed with a vaccination programme need not have been made as a single 'go'/'no go' decision. Rather, the decision process to implement the programme could have been segmented – the first decision being to place vaccination manufacturers on standby so that the rooster population was not culled, the second being to manufacture the vaccine, and the third being to proceed with the vaccination rollout itself. Thirty-three years later, reflecting on his role in the 1976 swine flu response, infectious disease specialist Edwin Kilbourne indicated that if he had his time again he would make the vaccine, promote the vaccine, but not give the vaccine until the last moment.

In theory, these decision points were still available to the 1976 vaccination programme as it was rolled out, but the early announcement by the president, that every man, woman and child would be vaccinated, made suspending the programme a less politically acceptable option. If, instead, the president had announced that they had committed funding to place manufacturers of vaccine on standby, and would make a decision by X date on whether it was necessary to proceed with vaccine production, they would have bought themselves valuable time to review their options as further information emerged.

Staged decision making was used to great effect by the University of Canterbury (UC) following the major earthquake in Christchurch.[7] As highlighted in Chapter 4, UC's greatest risk was student flight – whereby students would leave the city to study at another university. It needed to announce whether, and when, the university would reopen and teaching would begin for the new academic year.

The earthquake struck at lunchtime on Tuesday. During the first few days following the earthquake, the city was in chaos and people were in shock. As the week wore on, though, there was increasing pressure on the university to let people know if and when it would reopen. The university was stuck between a rock and a hard place. Students wanted certainty so that they could make their own decisions on whether to stay in or leave the city – they couldn't sit around and wait for a long time as available places at alternative universities would quickly fill up. But the university really had no sense at that time of how feasible it would be to reopen quickly. It had 240 buildings on campus. It would take days for engineers to check every building before they would know what they were dealing with. So, the university made an announcement that a decision on when it would reopen would be announced at 6 pm on Wednesday – eight days after the earthquake. Although it didn't know what that decision would be, it had just bought itself time to work it out.

Students now had certainty that they would have information to go on in just a few days' time, and the university had a valuable few days to undertake its impact assessment and to come to a decision. At 6 pm on that Wednesday, the university made its announcement that lectures would resume Monday week – three weeks after the earthquake. The university at the time of that announcement had little idea how it would achieve restarting teaching – but it now had 12 days in which to come up with a solution.

Incredibly, classes at the University of Canterbury did resume just three weeks after the devastating 22 February 2011 earthquake. With few buildings on campus able to be re-occupied, the university became creative – setting up large marquee tents to teach in, scaling up use of online teaching systems, and transforming its timetable to bring forward field trips and any other activities that could take place off-campus.

Reflecting on their experience, students talk about how hard that semester was. The tents were loud. There was a hard surface on the floors, which made it difficult to hear if anyone was moving about, and wind was also a problem. The tents were either boiling hot or freezing cold depending on the weather outside. But many students also talk about how these were some of the best courses of their degree. The students who stayed were the ones who really wanted to be there, creating a sense of resilience and success – and maybe even a little post-traumatic growth.

The concept of post-traumatic growth is an important one for resilience. Resilience is not just about surviving crisis – it is about finding ways to thrive. We often hear about people who completely re-evaluate their lives after a major health scare. The same can be true of organizations. Sometimes the best of opportunities can come from the worst of times. Hone your situation awareness to look also for the positives that might come from times of flux.

Look for the opportunity

When the Boxing Day tsunami struck southern Thailand in 2004, it came without warning. There was no major shaking felt – the earthquake was many thousands of kilometres away in Indonesia. There were also no warning systems in place to alert people to the devastation that was coming.

Just after 10 in the morning, the first sign of trouble was the sea retreating. Crabs and fish were left stranded on the sand. Some people recognized what this might mean, but many didn't – attracted onto the beach by this amazing phenomenon. And then came the wall of water.

I was a member of the New Zealand reconnaissance team sent to Thailand about four weeks after the tsunami, to understand and learn from the disaster.[8] The devastation we saw was immense. The water had reached the third floor of some hotels and had completely swept others off their foundations. The search for bodies was still ongoing – with photos of missing people everywhere.

Eight months later, I returned to Thailand to see how tourism was recovering. On some parts of the coast there were signs of renewal, as hotels reopened and tourists started to come back. Around Khao Lak, however, there were no such signs of recovery. Most of the damaged buildings had been cleared, leaving just desolated land. There were no tourists – just aid workers helping affected communities.

I was put in touch with a local tour guide to show me around for the day, and Kwan's personal story has stayed with me. The tsunami had taken nearly everything from her and had wiped out her thriving tour-guiding business. Some of her staff had lost their lives, most of her company's assets had been destroyed, and the social capital she had built up over so many years had been wiped out in an instant, with many friends and business associates either killed or moved away. Looking around Khao Lak, it was easy to see that the local area wasn't going to be a good location for a tour-guiding business any time soon.

So Kwan took a different tack. Looking around, she tried to find another business that she could run until tourists came back. The area was awash with aid agencies building new homes for the local community. The aid agencies were providing the houses, but few were providing furniture to fill those houses. Kwan had her idea. She opened up a furniture shop to provide her and her family with an income. She hadn't given up on her tour-guiding business – she would restart it in a few years' time, when the conditions were right.

Kwan is not alone in having to rethink her business following a major crisis. There are times when the crisis changes things so radically that what worked before will not work in the future. In these conditions, the most resilient response is not to doggedly reinstate your business, but to reinvent it.

Businesses that close following disaster are almost always invisible in post-disaster research. Their owners are often difficult to track down – many either moving away or going on to new ventures. And with no other information to go on, these organizations are often classed as 'failed businesses' that fell victim to the event. And yet this caricature masks a much richer reality. One of our researchers, Tracy Hatton, was interested to discover what happened to businesses that did not reopen following the Canterbury earthquakes.[9] She tracked down six businesses that were still closed two years after the earthquakes. Of the six, two went on to reopen a year later (three years after the earthquake), another two were still planning to reopen, and only two were permanently closed. Of the two permanently closed, only one could be considered to have 'failed', with the other choosing to remain closed and focus on other stores outside the impacted region.

Following a crisis is a time to refresh your situation awareness. Pause, take a deep breath and think, before leaping into response and recovery mode. Consider what has changed and re-evaluate what success might look like for your organization within this new environment. Don't just focus on one possible future for yourself and your business – explore several. A crisis provides a fleeting window of opportunity for transformative change. It is a time to take stock and re-evaluate priorities.

Summary

Here are some key take-outs from this chapter:

- Adversity may come from familiar sources or totally unexpected quarters.
- Turn your people into sentinels for the organization, always on the lookout for signals of change.
- Create mechanisms for gathering together all of that information and intelligence so that it can be understood in context.
- Develop a mindset within your team to explore alternative futures for how a situation could play out over time.
- Sometimes the best of opportunities can come from the worst of times – look for the positives that might come from times of flux.

Quick Start Guide: Sensemaking during rapid change

When your organization is in the midst of crisis, use these prompts as a regular touchstone to maintain your situation awareness:

Don't assume you know the full picture. Situations can change rapidly during a crisis and are often accompanied by confusion and communication breakdowns. Now is the time to ramp up your situation awareness capabilities. Draw together a horizon-scanning team to better understand your current situation, and what issues are likely to emerge in a day, a week, a month and a year's time.

Prepare for multiple futures. No one can predict the future, so don't lock onto a single scenario for how a situation might play out. Incorporate multiple scenarios into your planning approaches so that your plans are stress-tested against alternative futures.

Seek diverse perspectives. Draw on your networks to gather intelligence on what is happening and to stress-test your thinking and planning from diverse perspectives.

Buy extra time. Be strategic about what decisions need to be made by when. Being decisive doesn't mean you should lock yourself into a course of action too early. Break larger decisions into a series of smaller decisions, with clearly articulated timeframes or triggers for key decision points. This will give you more time to collect information and evaluate the options available to you. But, remember to make the decision when you said you would, or you will quickly erode trust.

Seek out opportunities. A crisis provides a fleeting window of opportunity for transformative change. It is a time to take stock and re-evaluate priorities. Think before leaping into re-sponse and recovery mode – where do you want your organization to be in five years' time? It might just be possible to fast-track that goal now.

Trust your gut. Crises don't always come with warning bells. If something doesn't feel right and you just have a bad feeling or hunch – don't dismiss it, investigate it. Our subconscious can often sense trouble far quicker than our conscious mind.

Resilience initiatives – improving situation awareness

Teams need practice at thinking through the multiple futures that different pieces of information might mean for the organization. This is a skill that can be learnt – but it takes practice. At the end of this book are a number of different initiatives that organizations can to use to improve their resilience. The initiatives with particular relevance for improving situation awareness are:

1	Get someone in to tell their story.
2	Take advantage of burning platforms.
28	Take the time to get to know people.
29	Actively scan the horizon.
30	Get people thinking beyond tomorrow.
31	Continually review your business model.
40	Get better at managing risk.
41	Learn from the past.
43	Practise decision making without all the information.
57	Manage change carefully.

References and further reading

A good way to find copies of academic papers is via Google Scholar: https://scholar.google.com.

1 Stuxnet:
- Zetter, K (2014) *Countdown to Zero Day: Stuxnet and the launch of the world's first digital weapon*, Crown, New York
- Kelley, MB (2013) The Stuxnet attack on Iran's nuclear plant was 'far more dangerous' than previously thought, *Business Insider*, 20 November, http://www.businessinsider.com/stuxnet-was-far-more-dangerous-than-previous-thought-2013-11
- Kushner, D (2013) The real story of Stuxnet: how Kaspersky Lab tracked down the malware that stymied Iran's nuclear-fuel enrichment program, *IEEE Spectrum*, 26 February, http://spectrum.ieee.org/telecom/security/the-real-story-of-stuxnet

– Rosenbaum, R (2012) Richard Clarke on who was behind the Stuxnet attack, *Smithsonian Magazine*, April, http://www.smithsonianmag.com/history/richard-clarke-on-who-was-behind-the-stuxnet-attack-160630516/?no-ist

– BSI (2014) *The State of IT Security in Germany 2014*, The Federal Office for Information Security in Germany (BSI), https://www.bsibund.de/SharedDocs/Downloads/EN/BSI/Publications/Securitysituation/IT-Security-Situation-in-Germany-2014.pdf?__blob=publicationFile&v=3

– KPMG Global Energy Institute (2013) *Energy at Risk: A study of IT security in the energy and natural resources industry*, KPMG, https://www.kpmg.com/Global/en/IssuesAndInsights/ArticlesPublications/Documents/energy-at-risk.pdf

– Mueller, RS III (2012) Combating Threats in the Cyber World – Outsmarting terrorists, hackers and spies, *RSA Cyber Security Conference*, San Francisco, CA, 1 March, https://www.fbi.gov/news/speeches/combating-threats-in-the-cyber-world-outsmarting-terrorists-hackers-and-spies

2 SARS:

– Huifeng, H (2013) When SARS first spread, Guangzhou residents sought out vinegar, *South China Morning Post*, 22 February, http://www.scmp.com/news/china/article/1155640/when-sars-first-spread-guangzhou-residents-sought-out-vinegar

– Loh, C (2004) *At the Epicentre: Hong Kong and the SARS outbreak*, Hong Kong University Press, Hong Kong

– Koh, T, Plant, A and Lee, EH (2003) *The New Global Threat: Severe Acute Respiratory Syndrome and its impacts*, World Scientific, Singapore

– Branswell, H (2008) SARS memories linger 5 years later, *The Ontario Star*, 6 March, http://www.thestar.com/news/ontario/2008/03/06/sars_memories_linger_5_years_later.html

– WHO (nd) *Update 95 – SARS: Chronology of a serial killer*, World Health Organization, http://www.who.int/csr/don/2003_07_04/en/

– Heymann, DL and Rodier, G (2004) Global surveillance, national surveillance, and SARS, *Emerging Infectious Diseases*, **10** (2), pp 173–75, http://doi.org/10.3201/eid1002.031038

– Forum on Microbial Threats, Board on Global Health, Institute of Medicine (2004) *Learning from SARS: Preparing for the next disease outbreak – workshop summary*, National Academies Press, Washington, DC

– Weinstein, RA (2004) Planning for epidemics – the lessons of SARS, *The New England Journal of Medicine*, **350** (23), pp 2332–34

– WHO (nd) *Alert and Response Operations*, World Health Organization, http://www.who.int/csr/alertresponse/en/

3 Encouraging the reporting of safety issues:

– Reason, J (1998) Achieving a safe culture: theory and practice, *Work & Stress*, **12** (3), pp 293–306

- O'Leary, M and Chaphall, SL (1997) Confidential incident reporting systems create vital awareness of safety problems, *ICAO Journal*, **51**, pp 11–13
4   Reason, J (1998) Achieving a safe culture: theory and practice, *Work & Stress*, **12** (3), pp 293–306
5   Turner, BA and Pidgeon, NF (1997) *Man-made Disasters*, Vol. 2, Butterworth-Heinemann, Oxford
6   1976 Swine flu:
   - Kolata, G (2011) *Flu: The story of the great influenza pandemic of 1918 and the search for the virus that caused it*, Farrar, Straus and Giroux, New York
   - Gaydos, JC, Top, FH, Hodder, RA *et al* (2006) Swine influenza A outbreak, Fort Dix, New Jersey, 1976, *Emerging Infectious Diseases*, **12** (1), http://dx.doi.org/10.3201/eid1201.050965
   - Sencer, DJ and Millar, JD (2006) Reflections on the 1976 swine flu vaccination program, *Emerging Infectious Diseases*, **12** (1), http://wwwnc.cdc.gov/eid/article/12/1/05-1007_article
   - Nelson, KE (2012) Invited commentary: influenza vaccine and Guillain-Barré Syndrome – is there a risk? *American Journal of Epidemiology*, **175** (11), pp 1129–32
   - Couzin-Frankel, J (2009) Retrospective: What happened with swine flu in 1976, *Science*, 25 April, http://www.sciencemag.org/news/2009/04/retrospective-what-happened-swine-flu-1976
7   Two books that provide further insights into the University of Canterbury's emergency preparedness and what helped them to recover from the Canterbury earthquakes are:
   - Seville, E, Hawker, C and Lyttle, J (2012) *Resilience Tested: A year and a half of 10,000 aftershocks*, University of Canterbury, http://www.canterbury.ac.nz/emergency/documents/resiliencetested.pdf
   - Seville, E, Hawker, C and Lyttle, J (2011) *Shaken but Not Stirred: A university's resilience in the face of adversity*, University of Canterbury, http://www.canterbury.ac.nz/emergency/documents/shakenbutnotstirred.pdf
8   Bell, R, Cowan, H, Dalziell, E *et al* (2005) Survey of impacts on the Andaman coast, southern Thailand following the great Sumatra-Andaman earthquake and tsunami of December 26, 2004, *Bulletin of the New Zealand Society for Earthquake Engineering*, **38** (3), pp 123–48, http://www.nzsee.org.nz/db/Bulletin/Archive/38(3)0123.pdf
9   Hatton, T (2015) *Collaborative Approaches to the Post-Disaster Recovery of Organisations*, PhD Thesis, University of Canterbury, http://www.resorgs.org.nz/Publications/collaborative-approaches-to-the-post-disaster-recovery-of-organisations.html

Learning organizations – moving to a mindset of constantly learning

06

When I was a kid, there was this TV programme called *MacGyver*.[1] Drawing on his vast knowledge of science and engineering, MacGyver was able get himself out of any seemingly intractable situation. He used whatever was around him. In one episode, for example, MacGyver managed to plug a sulphuric acid leak with chocolate. Sound far-fetched? Chocolate contains sucrose and glucose, and when the acid reacts with the sugars it creates elemental carbon and a thick gummy residue. The stunt was recently re-created on the TV programme *Mythbusters*, which proved it does, in fact, work.

MacGyver could get out of any situation. All he needed was his trusty pocketknife, a roll of duct tape and lots of ingenuity to use whatever resources he had to hand. Your organization needs to be like MacGyver – able to innovate and come up with practical solutions, whatever the situation.

A key ingredient in an organization's resilience is its levels of innovation and creativity – and this stems from its attitude to learning. Innovation and creativity are important for resilience, because the crisis that hits you inevitably won't be the one that you planned for. And even if you have planned for a particular type of event, in my experience real crises contain so many curve balls and surprises that the plan you have is unworkable. You need to develop the capability within your organization to 'build the plane while flying it'.

Innovation and creativity in an organization doesn't just emerge – it is a capability that needs to be nurtured. Innovation and creativity isn't something that should be isolated to the research and development arm of your organization (if you have one). Innovation and creativity needs to be baked into the way your organization approaches and solves challenges every day. It is a capability that is needed in every part of the organization and at all levels.

How well does your IT team solve issues? Do your admin staff take on new challenges and follow through until solutions are found? When there is a problem, does your senior management team pull together, or do they start finger pointing and assigning blame?

Innovation and creativity within an organization is as much about an attitude that embraces challenge, as it is about technical expertise. It requires curiosity and a can-do attitude. It requires teamwork and not being afraid of the first signs of failure. It is a capability that – if your organization has it – will improve performance during business-as-usual, as well as in times of crisis.

Like a plant, creativity and innovation requires the right ingredients and conditions to flourish.

Fostering innovation and creativity

In 2013, one of our researchers, Alia Bojilova,[2] was working as a military psychologist when she was selected to participate in a United Nations Truce Supervision (UNTSO) mission in the Middle East. There, she was deployed to Syria as an unarmed military observer. In May 2013, while at an observation post in the Area of Separation on the Syrian Golan Heights, the UN secure compound was breached. Alia and two others were confronted by a group of 38 armed men. They were taken at gunpoint, marched through minefields, and held hostage in a small remote village.

Alia and her colleagues were in real danger. Their captors told them they wanted to make a bad video of them, gesturing their thumbs across their throats. The group initially claimed to be members of the Syrian Army, but something about that didn't feel right. The group all had beards. In Alia's experience, most army recruits are clean shaven. Also, while the group was threatening very violent actions, something in their eyes told Alia they might not be committed to carrying out these acts. The stories of their captors kept changing, and their captors even staged a fake rescue attempt in an effort to create confusion and fear among the hostages.

While the situation was terrifying, Alia was also curious. The psychologist in her wanted to know what motivated her captors, what their views and objectives were and what they were like as people. She also needed to gauge what their real intentions were. Would it be possible to negotiate their way out, or would they need to focus on rescue or escape?

The situation could have had disastrous consequences. As hostages, Alia and her colleagues had to remain focused on the objective of getting out. Succumbing to fear would only have reduced their ability to reason, negotiate and find a solution that would get them home safely.

Alia knew from her training that the captors were trying to break them down mentally – wanting to exert power over the hostages so that they would be fearful, easier to handle and dehumanized. She knew that she had to maintain her self-respect and to be seen as an equal. This was especially important being a woman – she had to make it clear that she demanded respect as a UN officer.

Alia decided to follow her curiosity to see if she could learn more about their intentions. As she was led between two buildings, she saw a senior officer smoking. She asked him for a cigarette, which he gladly offered. The two talked about their families and where they each came from. This was an important moment. For Alia, it demonstrated that her captors were willing to open up and share information about their personal lives. From this, she knew that negotiation was a viable strategy for release.

Over the next hours, Alia and her team kept talking with their hostages, slowly demonstrating that they could be trusted partners in helping the group achieve its goals. It turned out that the group was a member of the Free Syrian Army (FSA) rebel group. During her time as a UN military observer, Alia had spent many hours observing the events that engulfed Syria and speculating what FSA members were like. She finally had an opportunity to find out first hand.

Alia had empathy for their cause. It emerged that what they really wanted to achieve through this whole incident was a face-to-face meeting with a senior UN official. The group had been trying to secure such a meeting for the past three years, but had been unsuccessful. Working together, Alia and her team managed to secure this meeting, successfully negotiating their release eight hours after being taken hostage.

Alia and her two colleagues were unharmed – but the event didn't leave them unchanged. They now had a deepened appreciation of the struggles, values and humanity of what could have otherwise been a group of dangerous and unpredictable hostage-takers. They also, unexpectedly, came away feeling that the kidnapping was an ultimately positive experience – having left with a renewed confidence in their abilities to negotiate in highly volatile and complex situations.

This experience led Alia to initiate the UNMO Resilience Project to help support incoming United Nations Military Observers to build their resilience by sharing reflections and coping strategies from those who had lived through significant critical incidents. Talking with military observers from around the world who had been deployed in Syria, Israel, Lebanon, Jordan and Egypt, a common theme emerged of what helps people to get through dangerous situations – their curiosity. 'At a time when your ability to control yourself and be optimistic is a matter of survival, you quickly learn that fear has nothing to offer. Your curiosity and commitment to reaching positive outcomes is all you can rest on and dedicate your energy to' (UN military observer kidnapped in Syria).

At the end of her deployment, Alia embarked on her PhD with us, to explore the link between the resilience of individuals and the resilience of the organization they work with. Focusing on the Special Forces, who are a specifically selected and trained elite division of the military, Alia again found curiosity coming to the fore. Curiosity was consistently cited as a decisive factor for success in Special Forces operations, where unconventional war space is the norm. As her Special Forces interviewees explained, without curiosity you can't envision your desired state or your path forward. Curiosity gives you the strength to deal with the unpredictable and the unknown.

Curiosity serves as a highly adaptive coping mechanism. It provides a shield from apathy, passive acceptance and despair, and is a strong contributing factor to active and effective engagement. Ultimately, Alia's work has revealed that curiosity is critical for achieving positive outcomes in situations of acute ambiguity and risk.

Resilience often requires adapting to a situation that is outside of your experience, and often outside of your plans. It requires your organization and your people not to be daunted by the unfamiliar and unexpected, but to be curious, actively exploring and experimenting to find new pathways through.

In 2012, a team of Resilient Organisations researchers, led by Venkataraman Nilakant and Bernard Walker,[3] set out to understand what enables some organizations to adapt quickly and discover new opportunity amid turmoil. Interviewing more than 200 senior managers from across the electricity, horizontal infrastructure, communication, transportation and banking sectors, they explored in depth the concept of 'adaptive resilience'. Adaptive resilience is highly dynamic, requiring the organization to be agile, coordinated and to learn rapidly. Their work identified four key requirements for an organization to achieve adaptive resilience – a culture of caring, a culture of sharing and a culture of learning, all underpinned by strong organizational leadership.

Collective learning and continuous improvement are central elements of the adaptive resilience model developed by Nilakant and Bernard's team. Organizations with a strong culture of learning are able to read new situations more accurately and keep adjusting their responses accordingly. The key elements they identified for this culture of learning include:

- an openness to learning, feedback and ongoing improvement;
- an environment that encourages problem solving rather than blaming;
- a 'safe' culture where it is OK to admit mistakes and jointly learn from them;
- an ability to pause and reflect, as individuals and as a group;
- an ability to listen to others and to consider alternative options;
- a willingness to take risks and explore untested new ideas.

Ever since Peter Senge's seminal work, *The Fifth Discipline*,[4] researchers around the world have been exploring the concept of what makes an organization a 'learning organization'. You can think of a learning organization as one that is skilled at creating, acquiring and sharing knowledge, ideas and insights, and using these to modify its behaviours.

Over the past two decades, researchers have taken Peter Senge's early ideas and delved further to see what drives an organization's predisposition to learn.[5] There are three broad factors essential for organizational learning and adaptability:

- leadership behaviour that positively reinforces the importance of learning for the organization;
- an environment where learning behaviours are actively encouraged, supported and enabled;
- concrete learning processes so that learnings become enacted and embedded into practice.

The injection of fresh ideas is essential if learning is to take place. We learn when we become aware of alternative ways of looking at an issue, sparking fresh thinking, energy and motivation. Sometimes new ideas are created through flashes of insight or creativity; at other times they arrive from outside the organization or are communicated by knowledgeable insiders. New ideas alone, however, do not lead to learning. An organization needs to be open-minded enough for these new ideas to challenge mental models and deeply held assumptions.

Successes and failures from the past all contribute to our understanding of how the world works. But as time passes, our current mental models become out of date. A learning organization has the courage to allow its established mental models to be tested, proactively questioning long-held routines, assumptions and beliefs. In many ways, you can think of learning as first requiring a commitment to unlearning – unlearning is at the heart of organizational change.

Organizational learning is strongly influenced by the behaviour of leaders. If leaders place little value on learning, or demonstrate an unwillingness to have their mental models challenged, learning is unlikely to occur. When leaders actively question – and listen – it shows a willingness to entertain alternative points of view. Employees in turn will feel emboldened to offer new ideas and options.

Systematic problem-solving, experimentation with new approaches, learning from the past, learning from others, and sharing that knowledge quickly and efficiently are all features of learning organizations. But these attributes alone do not create a learning organization. 'Lesson identified' is not necessarily the same as 'lesson learnt'. An organization must take its learnings and apply them.

It is surprisingly rare to find organizations that are good at applying lessons. Although organizations actively work hard to identify lessons, few learn them in a meaningful way. Many go on to repeat mistakes again and again. For learning to occur, an organization needs to be very intentional about taking lessons and actively embedding them in operational practice.

Marilyn Darling and her co-authors eloquently illustrate this point in their article 'Learning in the thick of it',[6] where they describe the After Action Review (AAR) process used by the US Army's Opposing Force (known as OPFOR). OPFOR is an army brigade with 2,500 members whose job it is to prepare soldiers for combat. OPFOR is designed to be the toughest of foes, taking on the role of 'the enemy' for mock campaigns against trainees who make up the Blue Force (BLUFOR). BLUFOR typically involves about 4,000 soldiers, many of them highly experienced on the battlefield.

BLUFOR is almost always better resourced and technically superior in every way; and yet OPFOR wins nearly every time. Why? Underlying the consistent success of OPFOR is the way it intentionally extracts lessons from every experience, and apply it into not just what it does, but also how it thinks.

OPFOR uses an AAR process, framed around four simple questions:

- What did we set out to do?
- What actually happened?
- Why did it happen?
- What do we do next time?

These sorts of question will sound familiar to anyone used to doing debriefs. But OPFOR uses After Action Reviews as far more than a debriefing process. The process is embedded within a highly intentional learning cycle that initiates from the very beginning of an exercise, and iterates through mini sensing, experimenting and adjustment cycles. Being intentional about learning is extremely powerful, and OPFOR demonstrates that this learning can take place at an organizational level.

To many people, learning, innovation and creativity are concepts associated with talented individuals. But researchers have been discovering that creativity can be a social process.[7] The next section explores why ideas carry more impact when they are co-created and shared widely.

Realizing the potential of co-creation

Doug Dietz is a design engineer who was super-proud of his new creation – a state-of-the-art MRI scanner.[8] Technicians and doctors all liked the new features and functionality of the machine. But one day, as Doug was walking out of a hospital, he turned to see a little girl, about seven years old, walking down the hallway with her mum and dad. As the little girl approached the MRI room, she burst into tears. Doug turned to look again at the MRI scanner he was so proud of. This time, he realized just how terrifying a contraption it was. For a little kid, being told to lie completely still while you are slowly sucked into a noisy machine must feel like being eaten alive. As a result, nearly 80 per cent of kids need sedating before they can be scanned.

For Doug, this was a heart-breaking realization. His machine, which he was so proud of, had completely failed to meet the needs of an important end-user group – sick children and their families. Doug and his team had been so focused on getting the 'technology' right that they hadn't really considered how patients would experience their design. Doug set about changing this – but to do that, he needed to get some different perspectives into the design process.

The concept Doug used to redesign his scanners was an approach called 'design thinking',[9] which shifts empathy for the user experience to be at the very heart of the design process. (More about design thinking and other techniques for breaking your thinking free is in the initiatives section at the end of this book.)

Doug didn't retreat into his lab to redesign the machine. He left the lab and spent time with preschoolers at his local daycare centre; he talked to child life specialists to understand what paediatric patients went through; he walked children through the MRI machine rooms to find out more specifically about what they found scary; he talked with experts from a local children's museum about how to capture a kid's attention and imagination. Then, drawing together these diverse perspectives, Doug's team set about redesigning the MRI experience.

The idea this new team developed was that small confined spaces aren't always scary for kids – but you have to harness their imagination. How many times have you seen kids transform 'three chairs and a blanket' into a play-hut? In their minds, this small space has become a castle, a fort, a pirate ship, or whatever sparks their imagination that day.

Knowing that he wouldn't be able to secure funding to completely redesign an MRI machine from scratch, Doug and his team instead transformed the MRI room so that the machine became part of a kid's adventure story. With colourful stickers applied to every surface of the room, covering the equipment, floor, ceilings and walls, and using music, lighting and fragrances to tap into all five senses, they set about capturing kids' imaginations.

There are now several different Adventure Series Scanners, ranging from pirate ship adventures to coral expeditions, space station missions and camping holiday trips. The MR Space Rocket was designed to incorporate the loud noises an MR scanner makes as the spaceship rumbles through space. In the Nuclear Medicine Jungle Adventure, the loading table becomes a canoe, which kids use to float down the river. If the kids lie really still, they can see fish jumping over the top of them. For little extra cost, creative thinking has transformed the experience for kids. The rate of young patients needing to be sedated in order to be scanned has plummeted.

Doug's positive experience of the benefits that come from getting others involved in the design process is not unique. There is something very powerful about the notion that complex problems can't be solved alone. By reaching out and engaging others in the process of both defining the problem and finding potential solutions, we are far more likely to get closer to a holistic solution.

Resilient organizations tend to have a 'one-in, all-in' culture; a culture where a problem is seen as 'our' problem and people all pitch in to resolve it. This is important, not only for the moral support it offers, but because it also leads to greater levels of innovation and creativity. When time pressures are on and the situation is both novel and complex, you need many minds working on the problem. Multiple perspectives are needed both to come up with ideas and to stress-test solutions. The solution that one team thinks is just perfect could have a glaring hole identified by someone with a fresh pair of eyes or a different perspective.

The very process of co-creation is empowering – it actively involves people in finding solutions. We all want to be part of the solution, not part of the problem. This is particularly true during times of crisis.

Just three months after the first devastating earthquake that shattered the city, Christchurch launched the Share an Idea campaign[10] to inspire the city's residents to envision what their city could become.

The campaign started with a really user-friendly website that crowdsourced ideas about how people wanted their city to be in the future. As people posted their ideas, these were categorized and almost immediately posted online. People could see not only their ideas but also those of others. Newspapers and advertising about the campaign showcased real ideas that had been submitted by the public – creating a sense that people's ideas were being heard. Best-of videos of submissions were created, which quickly spread via social media. This had a snowball effect. By showing people what ideas had already been submitted, they got even more ideas. The campaign gained momentum and people joined the conversation.

During the six-week consultation, one in five Christchurch residents participated, generating an astounding 106,000 ideas.[11] Ten thousand residents attended a weekend-long expo to discuss ideas for the future of the city. The campaign had people thinking about, and talking together about, the future of their city.

In the words of Christchurch's mayor: 'Share an Idea was designed not only to collect and process the best ideas from our people; it was also designed to replace our sense of powerlessness in the face of the earthquakes that shattered our city'.[12]

The concept of running a Share an Idea campaign isn't just relevant to a city struck by disaster. When the pressure comes on, organizations have a tendency to hunker down. They will often draw on a small, select team of people to problem solve, in the mistaken belief that engaging more people in the conversation will only slow them down. But think what your organization could achieve if it could stimulate, in a short period of time, the energy and ideas of all your people to finding a solution.

Action learning

A month or two after the first earthquake struck Christchurch, I was asked by City Care, a construction company, to come in and debrief their key staff. The purpose of these debriefs was to see what lessons might be learnt for how to improve their response 'next time' – not really thinking there would be a 'next time' quite so soon....

City Care has contracts to maintain considerable portions of Christchurch's water and wastewater networks, roads and parks, and as such it had a significant role to play in repairing and rebuilding the city's infrastructure.

The company swung into action immediately following the earthquakes, mobilizing support from right around the country to get basic services restored to city residents as quickly as possible. It is the first to admit that there were improvements needed, but, all in all, City Care performed remarkably well considering the scale of the task.

What I like about the City Care story is what it did next. It demonstrated that it was a learning organization; an organization that is constantly open and actively looking for ways to improve the way that it does things. In the months following the first earthquake, even though its workload was peaking, City Care took time to pause and reflect on its response to the earthquake. It considered, collectively, how it might do things better if there ever was a next time.

One source of learning for the team was how it nearly missed out on a major contract for the longer-term recovery and reconstruction. While it had been busy dealing with the immediate and urgent issue of reinstating essential services, it had underestimated the important, bigger-picture issues, such as by whom, and how, the longer-term reconstruction phase would be managed. The city had been divided into four rebuild areas – and City Care found itself with the smallest of these areas.

This is a common error that many organizations make during crisis response – they focus on the operational response, not seeing the strategic implications for the organization overall. Through the review we talked about how City Care could restructure its crisis response framework to create a distinction between the strategic and operational response teams, so that neither would be neglected.

Unfortunately for the city of Christchurch, City Care got to put its learnings into practice just six months later, when the city was struck by an even more devastating earthquake. City Care's response to this second earthquake was characterized by a much better balance between its strategic and operational priorities. The time it had invested in learning from its experience meant that it delivered a much smoother operational response. In addition, it also became a major player in the subsequent recovery effort, as a member of an alliance set up to manage the city's entire underground infrastructure rebuild.

While City Care's success at learning from its previous experience with disaster sounds like it should be obvious, it is remarkable the frequency that organizations just repeat the same mistakes time and time again. What makes City Care stand out is that it recognized the importance of immediately adjusting its practices with the new knowledge it had gained. This fast learn–adjust–monitor–review cycle meant that it was able to radically change its approach to the next crisis it faced.

In a world that is changing at a fast rate, our style of learning also needs to change. We aren't always going to have time to gather together the required knowledge and expertise before it is needed. We therefore need to get better at 'learning by doing'.

When you were learning to walk, you didn't achieve it by working out in advance what to do – instead you just 'did', discovering through trial and error what works and what doesn't. You also didn't let failure deter you – you just got back up and tried again with a few modifications to your technique. Learning to walk was a gradual process – first you learnt to roll over, then to crawl. Next, you discovered that you could pull yourself up on nearby tables and chairs, and pretty quickly you were taking your first steps, using these objects as your support. Finally, you were able to achieve a remarkable feat – to take your first steps unassisted. Within a few months you were off running.

The Red Cross recently put out a booklet on leading in times of chaos;[13] it makes the interesting observation that 'perfect' can be the enemy of 'good'. To allow creativity and innovation to flourish, we need to accept that we won't necessarily get everything right first time, and that failure is part of the learning process. By using techniques such as fast prototyping,[14] you can ensure that your failures do not have disastrous consequences.

A fast prototyping cycle is where we create something, and then get people to experience or use it and provide us with feedback. This feedback is then immediately incorporated into improving the prototype, which people use and again provide their feedback on. This cycle is repeated in quick succession to rapidly improve the quality of the prototype. A major benefit of the fast prototyping approach is that it creates a mindset that things are never going to be perfect from the start; it is a first iteration that should be tweaked and improved over time. With practice, this helps your organization to become more open to trying new things.

The idea of 'learning by doing' also points to the fact that in many cases, the people in the best position to come up with ideas for how to make improvements are those at the front line of your operations. Your own staff are often the best source of ideas for improvement. For example, the Clarion-Stockholm hotel in Sweden has implemented a number of measures to ensure it becomes an ideas-driven organization.[15] This four-star hotel in the centre of Stockholm averages about 50 ideas per year from each of its employees on ways to improve. That is an incredible number of ideas. The hotel uses a tool called C2 (Creative Culture) for employees to record ideas about how their work conditions, atmosphere and the hotel could be improved. It also collects ideas and complaints from its guests. Each department then has a weekly idea meeting to review all of the collected ideas and to decide what actions it wants to take. The interesting thing about this process is that it surfaces issues that wouldn't be readily identifiable by managers. For example, bar staff are the ones dealing with disgruntled customers who regularly misread the bar coupons given out to conference attendees – thinking they get a free drink rather than a discount on a drink. The idea to increase the font size on these coupons so that there is less confusion is both inexpensive and easy to implement. And this is just one example of an improvement suggested by staff. Fifty ideas for improvement each year from each staff member – that makes for a lot of ways to make the business better.

Southwest Airlines is another example of a company harnessing the power of many people's effort to find improvements.

In the early 1990s, Southwest Airlines had a problem.[16] Iraq had just invaded Kuwait, and fuel prices soared. The average monthly price of oil rose from $17 per barrel in July to $36 per barrel in October. Rather than just sweating over this fact among the executive team, Southwest's CEO Herb Kelleher sent a memo to pilots asking for their help. Pilots pitched in enthusiastically to design and implement a plan to reduce fuel consumption, and through inventive thinking, the pilots found ways to drop fuel consumption rapidly without compromising safety or service.

At the same time, about a quarter of employees at Southwest also banded together to create the 'Fuel from the Heart Program'. Through this programme, employees voluntarily donated from their pay cheques to buy gallons of fuel. While making only a small dent in the airline's $30-million/month fuel bill, this programme was instrumental in allowing employees to feel part of the solution.

In 2000, when fuel prices again began to skyrocket and the company needed to cut costs, Kelleher used the same strategy again. He sent a letter about the current fuel crisis to all of his employees – telling them that jet fuel was $1 a gallon, three times the previous year's cost. Southwest was using 19 million gallons a week. Explaining to staff that the company's profitability was in jeopardy, Kelleher asked each worker see if they could help by saving $5 a day. The response was immediate. One department offered to do its own janitorial work. A group of mechanics figured out how to heat the planes more cheaply. Within six weeks, employees had already saved the company more than $2 million. Over the next year, by each saving $5 a day, Southwest managed to cut costs by 5.6 per cent.

This collective response to a problem wasn't a one-off. The airline has actively fostered a culture of joint problem solving. For example, work is assigned in groups, and failure to deliver results is a 'team late'. Rather than assessing individual responsibility, teams are tasked to figure out how to avoid the problem in the future. The airline also has a 'Walk a Mile' programme, in which any employee can do somebody else's job for a day. There has been remarkable take-up – with 75 per cent of all staff participating in the job-swapping programme.[17] This has created an innate sense of teamwork towards problem solving, with pilots sometimes handling baggage or gate attendants helping to load provisions for a departing flight. Herb Kelleher, founder of Southwest Airlines, describes the programme as an administrative nightmare, but one of the best tools he knows of for building understanding and collaboration.

As this chapter has highlighted, to improve your organization's innovation and creativity requires a good attitude towards learning, and engaging diverse groups in the problem-solving process. In the same way that we can never see all aspects of a mountain just by standing in one place, we need to draw in alternative perspectives to find solutions for the challenges we face. Often, that process starts by recognizing the potential you already have within your organization for coming up with great ideas.

Summary

Here are some key take-outs from this chapter:

- Innovation and creativity in an organization doesn't just emerge – it is a capability that needs to be nurtured.
- Learning sometimes first requires unlearning. Be open-minded enough to allow new ideas to challenge mental models and deeply held assumptions.
- Organizational learning is strongly influenced by the behaviour of leaders. When leaders actively question – and listen – it shows a willingness to entertain alternative points of view. Employees in turn will feel emboldened to offer new ideas and options.
- 'Lesson identified' is not the same as 'lesson learnt'. Be very intentional about taking lessons and actively embedding them into operational practice.
- Complex problems can rarely be solved alone. Reach out and engage others in the problem-solving process – mobilize all your staff to identify things that could be improved.
- Failure is part of the learning process – iterate towards a better solution.

Quick Start Guide: Learning to build the plane while flying it

When your organization is in the midst of crisis, use these prompts as a regular touchstone to ensure you are thinking creatively enough about ways to address challenges:

Invite people to help.
Don't try to solve complex challenges on your own – reach out to others and ask them to help. Drawing together a diverse team will not only help to open up possibilities that you may not have thought of, but it will also mean you can stress-test options from multiple perspectives as you go.

Generate ideas.
Don't assume you already know the best solution. Consciously seek out alternative options or ways of doing things. Use rapid brainstorming cycles not only to source a large number of ideas, but also to stretch people into thinking more creatively.

Iterate towards the solution.
Don't get stuck trying to find the ideal solution. Accept that it may take a few iterations before you reach perfection. Follow a fast prototyping process; make a start, seek feedback and improve over time.

Change the venue.
Are your people feeling tired and out of ideas? Try changing location – there is nothing like working from somewhere different for the day to spark off your creative juices.

Learn from others.
While you may think that the situation your organization is facing is unique – trust me, it isn't. Someone, somewhere around the world will already have dealt with a challenge of a similar nature. Do a quick Google search to see what turns up. Also leverage your social capital – ask others to tap into their networks to see if people can suggest solutions.

Seek expert input.
Shortcut your way to solutions by asking someone who deals with this kind of problem all the time. They will be able to quickly map out a suite of possible solutions you could investigate.

Capture learnings for next time.
Every time you think 'if only we had…' or 'if only we could…', jot these ideas down. They are the starting point for your lessons learnt process. See if you can ensure that next time you can deliver on some of your wish-list.

Resilience initiatives – building innovation and creativity

At the end of this book are a number of different initiatives that organizations can to use to improve their resilience. The initiatives with particular relevance for improving organizational learning include:

4   Let it be their idea.

32   Co-create solutions.

33   Get people thinking outside the box.

34   Gather in more and better ideas.

35   Draw in fresh perspectives.

36   Go gravity-free.

37   Develop problem solvers in your team.

38   Is yours a learning organization?

39   Be intentional about learning lessons.

41   Learn from the past.

57   Manage change carefully.

References and further reading

A good way to find copies of academic papers is via Google Scholar: https://scholar.google.com.

1 MacGyver:
   - *MacGyver*, TV Series 1985–1992, http://www.imdb.com/title/tt0088559/
   - Mythbusters, *Can Chocolate Stop Acid*, http://www.discovery.com/tv-shows/mythbusters/videos/can-chocolate-stop-acid/

2 Alia Bojilova is part way through her PhD studies at the University of Waikato. Her thesis will explore the role that curiosity plays in resilience, with a particular focus on how these two concepts are enacted within the Special Forces within the military. Once published, a copy of Alia's thesis will be available on the Resilient Organisations theses page: http://www.resorgs.org.nz/Publications/research-theses.html

3 Adaptive resilience:
   - Walker, B and Nilakant, V (2015) *Building Adaptive Resilience: High-performing today, agile tomorrow, thriving in the future*, Resilient

Organisations Business Resource, ISBN 978-0-473-342, http://resorgs.org.nz/building-adaptive-resilience

- Nilakant, V, Walker, B, van Heugten, K *et al* (2014) Conceptualising adaptive resilience using grounded theory, *New Zealand Journal of Employment Relations*, **39** (1), pp 79–86, http://www.nzjournal.org/39(1)Nilakant.pdf
- Nilakant, V, Walker, B, Malinen, S *et al* (2016) Dynamics of organizational response to a disaster: a study of organizations impacted by earthquakes, in *Business and Post-disaster Management: Business, organisational and consumer resilience and the Christchurch earthquakes*, ed CM Hall, S Malinen, R Vosslamber *et al*, Routledge, London

4 Senge, PM (1990) *The Fifth Discipline: The art and practice of the learning organization*, Doubleday Currency, New York

5 Learning organizations and learning orientation:
- Calantone, RJ, Cavusgil, ST and Zhao, Y (2002) Learning orientation, firm innovation capability, and firm performance, *Industrial Marketing Management*, **31** (6), pp 515–24
- Garvin, DA (1993) Building a learning organization, *Harvard Business Review*, **71** (7), pp 78–91
- Garvin, DA, Edmondson, AC and Gino, F (2008) Is yours a learning organization? *Harvard Business Review*, **86** (3), pp 109–16
- Jackson, LM (2016) The influence of organisational culture on learning lessons: implementing a lessons management life cycle, *Australian Journal of Emergency Management*, **31** (1), https://ajem.infoservices.com.au/items/AJEM-31-01-06
- Sinkula, JM, Baker, WE and Noordewier, T (1997) A framework for market-based organizational learning: linking values, knowledge, and behavior, *Journal of the Academy of Marketing Science*, **25** (4), pp 305–18

6 After Action Reviews:
- Darling, M, Parry, C and Moore, J (2005) Learning in the thick of it, *Harvard Business Review*, **83** (7), pp 84–92, https://hbr.org/2005/07/learning-in-the-thick-of-it/ar/1
- Department of the Army (1993) *A Leaders Guide to After Action Reviews*, Training Circular 25-20, Headquarters, Department of the Army, Washington DC, http://www.au.af.mil/au/awc/awcgate/army/tc_25-20/tc25-20.pdf
- Salem-Schatz, S, Ordin, D and Mittman, B (2010) *Guide to the After-Action Review*, VA Center for Implementation Practice and Research Support, http://as.vanderbilt.edu/overview/faculty/facultycouncil/archive/sitemason.vanderbilt.edu/files/cHpJCw/Guide%20to%20the%20After%20Action%20Review.pdf

7 Creativity as a social process:
- Fedders, LE (2012) Creativity is a social process, *Science Nordic*, 9 August, http://sciencenordic.com/creativity-social-process

– Vangkilde, KT (2012) *Branding Hugo Boss: An Anthropology of Creativity in Fashion*, PhD Thesis, Department of Anthropology, University of Copenhagen

8 MRI Adventure Series:

– Dietz, D (2012) *Transforming healthcare for children and their families: Doug Dietz at TEDx, San Jose, CA 2012*, YouTube, https://www.youtube.com/watch?v=jajduxPD6H4&feature=youtu.be

– Kelley, T and Kelley, D (2013) *Creative Confidence: Unleashing the creative potential within us all*, Crown Business, New York

– GE (nd) *Adventure Series for Nuclear Medicine*, GE, http://www3.gehealthcare.com/en/products/categories/accessories_and_supplies/adventure_series_for_nuclear_medicine/jungle#tabs/tab84BA5A27B8D145F0A3C7257AA01A7C3F

9 Design thinking:

– d.school (nd) *d.school bootcamp bootleg*, Institute of Design at Stanford, http://dschool.stanford.edu/wp-content/uploads/2013/10/METHODCARDS-v3-slim.pdf

10 Share an Idea:

– CCC (nd) *Share an Idea*, Christchurch City Council, http://cccgovtnz.cwp.govt.nz/the-rebuild/strategic-plans/share-an-idea

– Tandem Studios (2014) *Share an idea – Community engagement in the rebuild of Christchurch's central city*, YouTube, uploaded 11 May 2014, https://www.youtube.com/watch?v=Y8rhXYAE-ZY

– Share an Idea (2011) *Share an Idea – Kids*, YouTube, uploaded 31 May 2011, https://www.youtube.com/watch?v=BK5AoTXjN34

11 Carlton, S (2013) Share an Idea, Spare a Thought: Community consultation in Christchurch's time-bound post-earthquake rebuild, *Journal of Human Rights in the Commonwealth*, **1** (2), pp 4–13

12 CCC (2011) Share an Idea wins International Award, Our Christchurch, http://resources.ccc.govt.nz/files/OurChch/ThePress20111126.pdf

13 McNaughton, E, Wills, J and Lallemant, D (2015) *Leading in Disaster Recovery: A companion through the chaos*, New Zealand Red Cross, http://www.resorgs.org.nz/Booklet-Guides/leading-in-disaster-recovery.html

14 Fast prototyping:

– Kelley, T (2001) Prototyping is the shorthand of innovation, *Design Management Journal (Former Series)*, **12** (3), pp 35–42

– Schrage, M (1993) The cultures of prototyping, *Design Management Journal (Former Series)*, **4** (1), pp 55–65

– Jones, M and Samalionis, F (2008) From small ideas to radical service innovation, *Design Management Review*, **19** (1), pp 20–26

15 Clarion-Stockholm Hotel:

– Robinson, AG and Schroeder, DM (2014) *The Idea-driven Organization: Unlocking the power in bottom-up ideas*, Berrett-Koehler, San Francisco

– Clarion Hotel (nd) *Enthusiastic Employees*, http://www.clarion.nu/enthusiastic-employees

16 Southwest Airlines:

– Kelleher, H (1997) A culture of commitment, *Leader to Leader*, **1997** (4), pp 20–24

– Brooker, K (2001) The chairman of the board looks back as Herb Kelleher hands over the controls, *Fortune Magazine*, 28 May, http://archive.fortune.com/magazines/fortune/fortune_archive/2001/05/28/303852/index.htm

– Muduli, A and Kaura, V (2011) Southwest Airlines success: a case study analysis, *BVIMR Management Edge*, **4** (2), pp 115–18

– Quick, JC (1992) Crafting an organizational culture: Herb's hand at Southwest Airlines, *Organizational Dynamics*, **21** (2), pp 45–56

– Karlsberg, R and Adler, J (nd) 7 strategies for sustained innovation, *Expert Performance Systems*, http://www.expertperformancesystems.com/reports/innovation_strategies.html

– Gwynne, SC (2012) Luv and war at 30,000 feet, *Texas Monthly*, March, http://www.texasmonthly.com/articles/luv-and-war-at-30000-feet/

– Gilbert, SJ (2009) *Come Fly with Me: A history of airline leadership*, Harvard Business School, Research and Ideas, http://hbswk.hbs.edu/item/come-fly-with-me-a-history-of-airline-leadership

– Gellene, D (1991) Southwest Air's employees pitching in on gas money, *Los Angeles Times*, 8 January, http://articles.latimes.com/1991-01-08/business/fi-7829_1_southwest-airlines

17 Kelleher, H (1997) A culture of commitment, *Leader to Leader*, **1997** (4), pp 20–24

The next tier of 07
resilience
ingredients

Within our Resilient Organisations model of resilience we have 13 indicators of resilience identified. Over the past five chapters, I have talked about the five most important elements required to create a resilient organization. I prioritized these five because I believe that if you get these right, the others are far more likely to occur also – naturally. For example, if you have very strong leadership within your organization, unity of purpose can flow from that. If you are good at creating and maintaining effective partnerships, this can compensate for a lack of internal resources. Similarly, if your organization has highly tuned situation awareness, it is more likely to plan and prepare for future potentialities.

While this prioritization is useful (it is much easier to focus on 5 areas rather than 13), organizations, like people, do not always behave like we might expect. There are many organizations that have a clear understanding of their major risks, but, for whatever reason, seem unwilling or incapable of preparing for them. Similarly, while your organization might have strong leadership, this leadership might be subdivided among a number of fiefdoms, so that within the organization there are silos emerging and parts of the organization uniting towards different purposes. The purpose of this chapter is to provide an overview of the remaining eight resilience indicators identified through our research:

- planning strategies;
- stress-testing plans;
- decision making;
- internal resources;
- leveraging knowledge;

- proactive posture;
- unity of purpose;
- breaking silos.

Planning for the unexpected

On 7 February 2008, 14 people were killed and another 36 were seriously burnt and injured in a disaster that should have never occurred – the Imperial Sugar explosions.[1]

In 2007, Imperial Sugar was one of the largest sugar refiners in the United States. Its manufacturing facility at Port Wentworth in Georgia was used to convert raw cane sugar into a variety of sugar products. Using a system of conveyors and elevators, sugar was transported through the factory. This was a fairly messy process. Significant quantities of sugar spilt onto the floors. It was sometimes piled knee deep, and one worker reported needing to use a squeegee to clear a path to the equipment he operated each day. It would be fair to say that housekeeping procedures at the factory were pretty poor.

The machinery within the factory also generated significant sugar dust. Sugar dust is well known to be dangerous. Way back in 1925, the book *The Dust Hazard in Industry* identified sugar, dextrin, starch and cocoa dusts as dangerous – and sugar dust exceptionally so. The problem with sugar arises when it is airborne. If a cloud of sugar dust reaches sufficient concentration and comes into contact with an ignition source, the resulting flame will travel throughout the dust-cloud with great rapidity. If this ignition takes place in a confined space, the pressures will cause explosive destruction.

Imperial Sugar's poor housekeeping practices had been a feature of its operations for many years, and although the issue had been raised repeatedly, corrective action wasn't taken. In 1967, an internal memo from a refinery engineer highlighted the need to remove heavy accumulations of dust. Just one year later, in September 1968, a dust explosion occurred inside the mill room. Refinery workers successfully extinguished the fire, but not before significant fire and smoke damage occurred.

In 1998, at a different Imperial Sugar refinery in Texas, an employee was severely burnt by a sugar dust explosion in the powdered sugar mill room. Yet, more than eight years after that incident, the corporate safety manager wrote in a memo that the company still did not have a formal policy for sanitation/housekeeping at any of its sites.

Then, in early 2008, there was a small explosion in a dry dust collector on the roof of the Port Wentworth packing building. Luckily, the collector was safely vented and so an explosion was prevented, but the dust collector was taken out of service.

At around the same time, Imperial Sugar hired an outside consultant to evaluate the dust collection systems. The report identified numerous design and maintenance deficiencies. The dust collection equipment was in disrepair; some equipment was significantly undersized; others were incorrectly installed. There were duct pipes completely filled with sugar dust. The consultant's report was delivered to Imperial Sugar management just a few days before disaster struck.

In 2007, Imperial Sugar had made a change. A stainless steel frame, with top and side panels, was installed to fully enclose each conveyor belt to protect the granulated sugar from falling debris. With the steel belts now enclosed, sugar dust was trapped inside – reaching explosive concentrations.

At around 7.15 pm on 7 February 2008, staff working at the Imperial Sugar facility were startled by what sounded like a heavy roll of packing material being dropped. An initial explosion of sugar dust had just occurred within one of the covered conveyor belts. As the pressure waves from this initial explosion swept through the plant, it disturbed settled sugar dust throughout the factory. Many years' worth of accumulated dust on beams and rafters in the roof area was thrown into the air. Three to five seconds later, this sugar dust ignited. Massive flames and debris erupted above the packing buildings and silos. Within the facility, three-inch-thick concrete floors heaved and buckled from the force of the explosions as they spread from the packing buildings and into adjacent buildings.

Workers in the packing buildings had little or no warning as walls, equipment and furniture were thrown about. Superheated air burnt workers as they tried to escape. Debris littered the passageways and some exits were blocked. The fire sprinkler system failed because the explosions ruptured the water pipes.

The piles of granulated and powdered sugar that had accumulated around equipment intensified the fires. Explosions travelled through the enclosed conveyors to ignite fires in other buildings, hundreds of feet from where the incident had begun. For more than 15 minutes, violent fireballs erupted from the facility.

The Imperial Sugar disaster was completely preventable and is a dreadful illustration of the devastation that can be wrought by a failure to adhere to robust operating discipline. It highlights two important indicators of resilience: the way an organization approaches planning, and the extent to which it stress-tests those plans.

Planning strategies

When talking about the planning strategies indicator within our organizational resilience framework, people often think we are referring to an organization's crisis and emergency response plans, or its business continuity planning approaches. While these specific plans are very important from a resilience perspective, the planning strategies indicator doesn't just refer to these. This indicator looks more holistically at how an organization undertakes planning in general – we are interested in the organization's operational discipline.

I was first introduced to the concept of operational discipline while visiting the headquarters of American conglomerate DuPont in 2008. I was walking down a flight of stairs beside Jim Porter, Chief Engineer and Vice President of Engineering and Operations for DuPont, when he turned to me and asked that I hold the handrail. Taken aback, I quickly complied.

Jim explained that DuPont has a policy that everyone should have two points of contact at all times while going up or down stairs, to help prevent slips, trips and falls. Throughout the rest of the day, a consistent theme emerged from every DuPont employee I met – that doing things the right way, every time, was not optional – it was the only way things should be done. I was even more amazed to learn that it could be a dismissible offence to be caught driving on company grounds without a seatbelt on – I had never heard of an organization taking health and safety so far.

DuPont has gone to great lengths to ensure that operational discipline is at the very heart of its organizational culture. Simply put, operational discipline means complying with a set of well-thought-out and well-defined processes, and consistently executing them correctly every time. DuPont says it is its way of driving towards operational excellence.

Effective operational discipline is a strong feature of high-reliability organizations, operating within high-risk industries, such as nuclear power or aviation. In these industries, the consequences of an accident can be so catastrophic that they need to achieve error-free operations.

DuPont began operations in the 19th century as a gunpowder manufacturer – arguably the highest-risk industry of the era.[2] The company is now over 200 years old. Right from the time the company was founded, a standard was set to create a culture of safety. Pierre du Pont built his home above the black powder mill – the closest house to the mill. That sent a powerful message about caring about safety and people. If there was an explosion, he was going to feel it first. The company had written safety rules as early as 1811.

In 1818, while members of the du Pont family were away, there was an explosion at the factory that killed 34 people.[3] After that, anytime there was a new formulation of powder, a member of the du Pont family had to be present during the testing process. If it wasn't safe enough for a family member, it wasn't safe enough for an employee.

To this day, DuPont executives maintain that their operating discipline doesn't just have safety benefits – it also provides more predictability across their organization. They can reach higher levels of efficiency, experience fewer mistakes and improve quality. Having strong operational discipline is all about doing the basics right. This is so important from a resilience perspective, as it means that your organization is going to be less crisis-prone.

Stress-testing plans

Planning is all very well, but truly resilient organizations are also constantly mindful of the limitations of their planning. They will actively seek out evidence that their assumptions are wrong.

Plans that haven't been actively stress-tested can be thought of as 'fantasy plans' – plans that look on paper to have everything sorted, but in reality are ineffective or simply not practical. There is a saying that no plan survives its first activation, but the very least you can do is to try to find its most vulnerable points in advance of a crisis. The sources of this vulnerability can be surprising. For example, following Hurricane Andrew in 1992, telephone companies discovered that the critical chokepoint in restoring service was not the poles, wires and switches that it had stockpiled in anticipation of a disruption, but the need for daycare centres.[4] Many of the phone companies' field operations employees had children and relied on daycare. When the centres were destroyed by the hurricane, someone had to stay at home to take care of the children. This meant that the workforce, whom the companies were relying on, suddenly wasn't available. The companies eventually managed to solve the problem by finding retirees to tend ad hoc daycare centres, thereby freeing working parents to assist in restoring the telephone network.

Preparedness takes practice. Teams don't fall smoothly in place on the day of a disaster, and no crisis response will ever run as smoothly as you planned. If you train your staff, actively stress-testing your plans and your response capability, you will build the fundamental skills and operating disciplines to cope with whatever comes along. For ideas on how to do this, take a look at the initiatives section at the end of this book.

Adapting ways of operating

An unfortunate reality is that the future just isn't that predictable. Yet many of our traditional business processes are designed around reducing uncertainty, so that our business tools and techniques are capable of managing them. But what happens when this is not possible? The world is becoming so complex that we need new ways of approaching problems – techniques that can accommodate uncertainty and complexity rather than needing to suppress them.

To illustrate this point, the World Bank[5] is exploring ways to reframe the way we make investment decisions about climate change adaptation. Climate change, and what to do about it, is a field characterized by deep uncertainty and complexity. Scientific consensus is emerging that the planet is warming owing to greenhouse gas emissions, but there is still significant disagreement between models and experts on what that means for the future climate in any particular region, or the specific effects that climate change will have on different sectors and groups. As climate science continues to develop and our knowledge improves, some of this uncertainty will dissipate. Other aspects of it, however, may actually increase. If an organization or community wants to invest in mitigation and adaptation to the effects of climate change, this uncertainty can quickly become a barrier to action. We all want confidence that our resources will be spent wisely, and it is unsettling to think that we are not even totally sure what the effects are that we need to mitigate against.

As the World Bank and others point out, traditional decision processes ask us to first reduce uncertainty by agreeing on assumptions about current and future conditions, which can then be used in our analysis to find an optimal solution. While sensitivity analyses will usually be run to assess the effect of changing assumptions, the underlying premise of this decision evaluation approach is that we can, broadly, forecast what the likely future conditions will be.[6]

And yet the premise that we can effectively forecast future conditions has very shaky foundations. There are just so many things that create non-linear effects in our highly complex and interrelated world. The research literature abounds with evidence that our predictions of the future are often wrong. For example, prior to the 1970s, the rate of oil consumption was rising at a very steady (and predictable) rate. A century's worth of data suggested a direct relationship between gross national product and energy consumption. The 1973 oil shock, however, triggered innovation and radical behavioural and policy changes. This led to large increases in energy efficiency that would have been inconceivable prior to the oil shock, and set our oil usage future on an entirely different course.[7]

Economic forecasting is another case in point. For all of the effort invested, it is still a highly unreliable endeavour.[8] The US Federal Reserve surveys professional economic forecasters each year to get their projections for the next year's change in GDP. In the 18 years from 1993 to 2010, the actual GDP fell outside the 90 per cent confidence interval of their predictions six times – three times as often as it should have, if the projections offered a true 90 per cent confidence interval.[9] Other researchers have looked at the usefulness of the forecasts published in the *Wall Street Journal* by prominent analysts. Looking at their forecasts for interest rates just six months into the future, these researchers found that while there was generally consensus among the analysts as to the likely movement of both short- and long-term interest rates, their predictions were no more accurate than a random number generator predicting incremental changes over time would have been.[10]

If the art of forecasting is fraught even for experts whose entire careers have been based on it, you can almost bet that your organization also won't get it right in predicting the future it needs to prepare for. This means that we need to develop new ways of thinking and working that does give your organization ways to survive, thrive and find opportunities in any future that you might face.

I currently lead a team of researchers within QuakeCoRE,[11] a Centre of Research Excellence on earthquake resilience, trying to understand, as a nation, how New Zealand might best improve its resilience to earthquakes. The challenge is that there are many different ways to improve resilience, but we don't have sufficient time, energy or resources to do all of them. We therefore need to prioritize where to put our efforts. But deciding between different resilience pathways is difficult, because it can be like comparing apples with oranges.

For New Zealand, there are many different resilience strategies we could pursue to make our communities more resilient to earthquakes. For example, we could use legislation and change the building codes to require all new and upgraded buildings to be built to a better standard; alternatively, we could provide incentives for building owners to improve the strength of their buildings; another option could be to change land-use planning rules to ensure that development does not occur in the highest -risk areas; or we could invest in better governance so that resilience becomes 'baked in' to the way our communities operate; or we could invest in reducing poverty, improving education and enhancing social capital within our communities; or we could focus on improving our ability to rebuild and recover from earthquakes better and faster.

Each of these measures, in its own way, would deliver a tangible improvement in our resilience to earthquakes. Some have very long lead times before they become effective; if an earthquake occurs before they have time to take effect, the investment may have limited payback. Others, however, deliver positive benefits even if an earthquake doesn't occur.

A traditional decision evaluation approach would have us evaluating the likelihood of an earthquake occurring within the agreed decision timeframe, and evaluating the costs and benefits that would be incurred and accrued with and without the investment. But most of our analysis would be based on a risk-based 'business-as-usual' view of New Zealand's exposure to earthquake risk. But what happens if our country enters an unusually quiet seismic period for the next 50 years and there are very few earthquakes: which resilience investments would look like the better investment in that case? What happens if things start getting very shaky for us and we get a series of earthquakes affecting different regions around the country in quick succession – which resilience strategies will enable our nation to get through? Either of these futures is perfectly feasible for our country – and yet they would each point to a very different suite of resilience initiatives as being the best investment.

What happens if conditions change radically before the next earthquake? In New Zealand, commercial and residential insurance for earthquakes is readily available and relatively cheap at present. That is not the case in many earthquake-prone countries. What happens if earthquake insurance in New Zealand becomes much harder or expensive to get? This could radically change the benefit–cost profile for many resilience investments.

What these examples highlight is that resilience requires us to adjust our thinking to better cope with the complexities we now face. Many of our standard business tools and practices are not designed to work well under conditions of deep uncertainty. What we need to do is to develop new ways of doing things that will identify strategies that are robust and perform well, no matter what the future brings. Here are some ideas for how you might go about this in relation to the next three resilience indicators: decision making, internal resources and leveraging knowledge.

Decision making

The way your organization makes decisions has a significant influence on its resilience. There are some organizations that analyse things intensely and become stuck in 'paralysis by analysis'. Other organizations are more 'shoot from the hip' in their decision-making style and therefore make silly mistakes. I have also seen organizations that completely flip their decision-making style during a crisis – throwing away their traditional decision-making practices for something completely new, and not always for the better.

In the same way that there is no one leadership style that is ideal for re-silience, similarly there is not one perfect decision-making style that all organizations should try to adopt. Instead, here are some principles for adapting your organization's natural decision-making style to make it more primed for resilience:

- **Always consider multiple options:** Researchers[12] looking at decision making have made a surprising discovery – fast decision makers don't achieve their speed by narrowing their focus. Instead, they consciously consider a number of alternative options before making a choice. Some will even throw their support behind options that they don't actually like, to trigger debate and provide contrast.

    Why is the analysis of multiple alternative options faster than just considering one or two? The reason is that contrasting alternatives can make it easier to identify points of difference and superiority. For ex-ample, if you are going to buy a new car, it can be difficult to sit down and specify (beyond the abstract) exactly what you want in a car. However, go and test-drive five different cars and it pretty soon clarifies your thinking. You soon get to understand the inherent trade-offs you need to make between fuel efficiency, looks, comfort and performance. By seeing what you don't like about something, it helps you to clarify what you do like and where your priorities lie.

    There are two other important benefits that come from comparing multiple alternatives concurrently. First, it is confidence building. You are far more likely to back your decision having looked at a range of potential options than you are if you have only really explored one option in depth. The second reason is that it means that if your preferred option doesn't work out for any particular reason, you have already done the analysis on a backup alternative. This helps to avoid becoming 'locked on' to a single course of action, pursuing it relentlessly, long after its flaws have become obvious.

- **Stress-test options from diverse perspectives:** While urgent decisions sometimes need to be made without consultation, even in a crisis those situations are few and far between. Inevitably, the decisions that go wrong tend to be the ones that are taken by one person, unilaterally. All decisions need stress-testing, even if that is as simple as bouncing it off one or two trusted people to get their views. Even better is to ensure that you have a team of good people behind you; people who will support you but who will also provide constructive critique and challenge. Someone with a background in HR is going to look at the problem from a people/capability/employment perspective; others with a marketing/sales perspective will focus on implications for customers etc. By seeking out different perspectives on your problem (and potential solutions), it offers new perspectives – so you are seeing the challenge from another angle.

- **Seek robust solutions:** Beware of brittle decisions – ones that are optimal for a particular set of assumptions, but which perform poorly or even disastrously under other assumptions. Resilience requires us to identify and adopt strategies that are robust in the face of the inevitably imperfect and uncertain forecasts of the future. Adjust your decision-making criteria to favour options that perform well across a wide range of futures.

- **Ensure the right people are involved:** In the US Navy, every sailor on the deck of an aircraft carrier is responsible for halting flight operations if he or she sees anything amiss. It doesn't matter what their level of seniority is – if they see something they that could jeopardize safety, then they have a delegated authority to act.[13] In a crisis, communication almost always deteriorates. You therefore need to empower your staff to make decisions and to take action, without always having to ask permission first.

Over the course of the next month, take notice of who in your organization is making decisions on what, and then review if the levels are calibrated right. If your senior management team is often discussing and deciding on quite low-level issues, think about ways to encourage them to delegate these decisions to their staff. If your lower-level staff are regularly making decisions that should really have visibility of more senior managers, ponder why this might be. Are managers so busy that there are few opportunities for staff to present issues or options for their manager's review? Are staff intentionally not escalating issues because they are worried about undue interference? A little bit of time spent getting agreement on who has the ability to make which decisions under different circumstances is a great way to empower your staff and free up managers for tackling the really big issues.

More ideas on decision-making techniques that work well in conditions of rapid change and deep uncertainty are provided in the resilience initiatives chapter at the end of this book.

Internal resources

It can be very tempting to think that the future is highly predictable, and therefore we can optimize the amount of resources (staff, spares of equipment, stock, credit etc) required to keep our business operations running smoothly. But, in the same way that your parents probably told you to save for a rainy day, it is important for your organization to have access to additional resources should things not go to plan.

This doesn't necessarily mean that you need lots of spare resources sitting around being underutilized. There are many different ways of managing your organization's resources to improve resilience. Here are just some of the ways you might expand the capacity of your resources. I've provided examples of how these principles might apply to your people resources – but the same principles can equally be applied to any other resource type.

- **Design in resilience**: design your systems and processes with resilience in mind so that they are less likely to cause you issues. For example, from a people perspective, don't constantly work your staff at 120 per cent capacity – it will just make your organization more vulnerable to issues associated with burnout and poor performance.

- **Have spare capacity**: If there are some resources that are critical to your operations, ensure you have spares on hand or know where to get them quickly. While you can't clone your best people, you can undertake succession planning and ensure that more than one person can fill key roles.

- **Have workarounds**: Consider whether there are alternative ways of getting the job done if required. For example, if your building is inaccessible, can your people work from elsewhere, such as home or an alternative site?

- **Redeploy existing resources:** Shift resources from one part of your organization to another as priorities shift. For example, if there is flu going round and half of your staff are off sick, then don't just work your remaining staff twice as hard. Otherwise they will just get sick too. Take a hard look at everyone's workload. Decide what is top priority and give people permission to defer or leave lower-priority tasks.

- **Draw in support from outside:** There will be times when the need for resources outstrips what you can supply from inside the organization, so consider ways to rapidly source and integrate resources from outside your organization. For example, if you need 10 more IT people at short notice, think about whom you might approach to find that extra resource. For example, could you use subcontractors or have mutual aid agreements in place to share staff via secondment or other arrangement?

While the above examples focused on people, there are many other internal resources your organization needs to operate. Knowing what is essential to keep your business going and how to achieve it is at the core of a business continuity plan. For more information on developing a business continuity plan, see the resilience initiatives chapter at the end of this book.

For many organizations, insurance is an important mechanism for financing the replacement of resources that have been lost or damaged through an unexpected event. It is important to know, however, that insurance is not a panacea that will fully compensate your loss. Large insurance claims are inevitably complex and take significant time and energy to negotiate. They can also take a long time to settle. For tips on how to ensure that your insurances are fit for purpose and will really help you out when you need it, take a look at the insurance initiative in the resilience initiatives chapter at the end of the book.

Leveraging knowledge

I have already touched on the need to leverage knowledge several times in this book, so will give only a brief description here. The leveraging knowledge indicator is all about ensuring that the knowledge your organization already has is both protected and accessible, so that it really can be used to full advantage by the organization. This knowledge includes data, information, key skill-sets, institutional memory, tacit knowledge, experience, and expertise. It also requires knowing when your organization is out of its depth and should draw in expertise from outside to help.

Being able to do these things effectively is strongly related to how engaged your staff are (Chapter 3), your ability to tap into social networks to draw in support (Chapter 4), the way information flows within your organization (Chapter 5) and your organization's openness to different perspectives (Chapter 6).

An ethos of resilience

'Our mission is to not get MOCHED.' This is the message that one critical infrastructure provider CEO gave to each and every new recruit when they started with the company. MOCHED (pronounced 'mocked') stands for Major Outage Causing Huge Economic Disruption. For this CEO, it wasn't the everyday kind of risks that kept him awake at night; he had his eye on the risks with unbearable consequences for both his community and his company.

Something as simple as a CEO's chats to new recruits has a powerful effect – they establish over time an organizational culture focused on resilience. Whether it is an acronym like MOCHED or some other mechanism, it is important to find ways to engage people across your organization in the re-silience conversation.

There is something very powerful that comes from having resilience thinking baked into your organization's DNA. A resilience culture moves far beyond just developing good crisis plans and running exercises; it is about developing a mindset and an attitude, right across your organization, that the world is likely to change in ways we don't expect, so there is both the need and imperative to be ready. The next three indicators are all about de-veloping an underlying ethos within your organization that enables it to pull together and face up to challenges.

Proactive posture

For your organization to be resilient, it needs a proactive posture. This is a strategic and behavioural readiness to respond to early warning signals of change – before they escalate into crisis. Proactive posture is highly related to your organization's situation awareness, but focuses more on your organ-ization's willingness to translate awareness into action.

Being proactive means thinking ahead, anticipating, planning and preparing for the future. This takes time and dedicated effort. How often do people within your organization step back from their day-to-day roles to take stock, review how things are performing, and to think creatively about what the future may bring and what they might do about it?

A common piece of advice given to small business owners is that they need to take time out from working *in* their business, so they can work *on* their business. This advice is equally relevant for people working in larger organizations. If you constantly have your head down, focusing on the problems and issues of today, you might not see the future coming. Take time to pause, look up, see where you are going, and change direction if you need to.

Unity of purpose

I once did some work with a construction company that struck me as just the sort of team you would want on your side if there ever was a problem. Its very strong unity of purpose stood out. Talking with the senior managers of this organization, they could very clearly articulate what the organization's top priorities would be during a crisis. Talking with the construction crews, they used different words, but essentially they told me exactly the same thing. And people in the organization believed in that core mission intensely. You could be sure that when they were needed, those crews would be mobilizing before they were asked.

When your organization is struck by a crisis, would everyone within your organization pull in the same direction? Does your team have a collective goal that you are all working towards? Great things can be achieved when people are all working together. To win in a tug of war, everyone has to pull straight backwards. If some people pull slightly to the left and others to the right, it means that they are working against each other, not together. If you can add in someone chanting 'pull, pull', it helps everyone to synchronize their efforts, creating a greater force to pull the other team over the line. This is what unity of purpose is all about – ensuring that your people all have a shared understanding of where they are heading, and are working together rather than against each other, to achieve that goal.

Unity of purpose sounds simple in theory, but is surprisingly difficult to achieve in reality. During times of crisis, your organization will need to make some tough decisions – prioritizing some goals, while setting others aside for the meantime. For staff whose day-to-day role was all about delivering these now lower-priority tasks, this can be hard to accept. Whether these staff will put their heart and soul into helping achieve the new priorities depends on both the quality of your leadership and the level of engagement they have with the organization and team.

Breaking silos

If you look at a common organizational chart from a distance, it can look like a series of grain silos stacked alongside each other. There is linkage across the top created by the senior management team, but then each member of the senior management team essentially has control over their own domains or hierarchy that reports to them. This representation is, of course, a simplification. In reality, organizations don't really operate as statically as would be indicated by their organizational chart, but it is a useful analogy. Silo mentality within an organization occurs when a team or part of an organization becomes inwardly focused, prioritizing the goals of the team over and above broader goals of the organization.[14] This can occur for any number of reasons, ranging from power-hungry leaders wishing to create their own little fiefdom, through to more inane reasons, such as teams never getting to meet each other because they are in different offices or located in different parts of the world.

Silos can arise within organizations, between organizations, and between disciplines (eg engineers vs accountants). They are a cultural phenomenon that relate to human behaviour. You can diagnose a silo mentality when there are different camps emerging in your organization, with 'us and them' attitudes. If you have ever heard a team moaning about another team within your organization, making it sound like they are the 'opposition' rather than on the same team, you know you have a problem.

Silos can be very detrimental to an organization. They lead to breakdowns in communication, cooperation and coordination, and result in fragmented effort. If your organization doesn't play as one team during business-as-usual, you can't expect people to start playing nicely together during times of crisis. Teamwork is a skill that needs to be developed and practised. To foster relationships and create bridges across organizational silos, I suggest being intentional about creating a work environment that brings people together, and rewarding collaboration and positive behaviours. The ways you can create better connections within your organization are endless. A good way to start is to regularly use cross-organization teams to solve business-as-usual problems.

Being connected and working together well is so important for resilience because there is always an inevitable surge in workload that accompanies times of rapid change and crisis. People from right across the organization need to pitch in to help those who are most affected. While it may seem obvious that a whole-of-organization response is needed during a crisis, it doesn't always occur. We see examples time and time again, where one department is struggling to cope with a major situation that is unfolding around them, while the rest of the organization continues on oblivious, often still demanding they deliver their day-to-day activities such as submitting timesheets on time. If you can get your organization working together as an effective team, you are well on your way to becoming more resilient.

Summary

Here are some key take-outs from this chapter:

- Instil a strong operating discipline in your organization. Do the basics right and your organization will be less prone to crises.

- Preparedness takes practice. Train your staff and actively stress-test your plans and response capabilities to build the fundamental skills and operating disciplines to cope with the unexpected.

- Given that the future isn't particularly predictable, practise decision-making techniques that select options that are robust and perform well, no matter what the future brings.

- Think creatively about how you can manage, expand and flex your organization's resources if required to meet rapidly changing needs.

- Ensure that the knowledge your organization already has is both protected and accessible, so that it can be used to full advantage in times of crisis.

- Be proactive in thinking ahead, anticipating, planning and preparing for the future. Take time to pause, look up, see where you are going, and change direction if you need to.

- During times of crisis, your organization will need to make some tough decisions – prioritizing some goals, while setting others. Ensure your people have a shared understanding and work together to achieve that goal.

- Silos can be very detrimental to an organization. Be intentional about creating a work environment that brings people together. Reward collaboration and positive behaviours.

Quick Start Guide: Other things to watch for

When your organization is in the midst of crisis, use these prompts as a regular touchstone to ensure you are on track:

Articulate your goals.	People can't help you achieve your goals if they don't know what they are. Take the time to clarify what you want to achieve and why – and then tell others who need to know.
Be ready for surprises.	Don't just plan for the expected – be ready for the unexpected too. Always consider the multiple possible ways that a scenario could play out. Try to find solutions that are robust across diverse conditions.
Appreciate alternative perspectives.	Draw together diverse teams to stress-test ideas and to come up with new solutions. Form teams around specific problems rather than areas of expertise – this way you encourage cross-disciplinary and cross-team collaboration, enabling a broader mix of people with a stake in the problem to be involved in designing the solution.
Review, reprioritize and redeploy.	Break free from business-as-usual thinking and ways of doing things. In a crisis you need to be responsive, agile and adaptable. If your usual way of doing things isn't going to be sufficient, come up with new ways to get things done.
Get ahead of the crisis.	While today's challenges might seem enough, I'm afraid tomorrow will bring a whole new set of challenges. A crisis situation will always evolve. Like a chess player, you need to think several moves ahead. What will probably be your big issues tomorrow, next week, next month? What can you do now that will put you in a better position to deal with them when they do arise?

Resilience initiatives

At the end of this book are a number of different initiatives that organizations can to use to improve their resilience. The initiatives with particular relevance for planning for the unexpected, adapting ways of operating and developing an ethos of resilience are:

40   Get better at managing risk.

41   Learn from the past.

42   Develop plans with your team.

43   Practise decision making without all the information.

44   Practise 'activating' a crisis response.

45   Print out the Quick Start Guides.

46   Regularly test your emergency plans.

47   Prepare for recovery, not just response.

48   Run exercises with other organizations.

49   Socialize your plans.

50   Map your staff vulnerabilities.

51   Ensure you have funds set aside for a 'rainy day'.

52   Get the most out of your insurance.

53   Make sure you can contact people.

54   Prepare key communications messages in advance.

55   Use crisis response capabilities to deal with everyday business challenges.

56   Develop good decision-making practices.

57   Manage change carefully.

58   Have good succession planning.

59   Focus on knowledge transfer gaps.

60   Encourage cross-department working.

61   Practise change.

62   Develop more flexible work practices.

63   Make resilience an organizational goal.

64   Embed core values in day-to-day operations.

65   Build a culture of optimism.

66   Maintain a strategic focus.

References and further reading

A good way to find copies of academic papers is via Google Scholar: https://scholar.google.com

1 Imperial Sugar disaster:
    – U.S. Chemical Safety and Hazard Investigation Board (2009) *Investigation Report: Sugar Dust Explosion and Fire, Imperial Sugar Company, Port Wentworth, Georgia, February 7, 2008*, Report No. 2008-05-I-GA, September 2009
    – Gibbs, WE (1925) *The Dust Hazard in Industry*, Ernest Benn, London
    – Vorderbrueggen, JB (2011) Imperial Sugar refinery combustible dust explosion investigation, *Process Safety Progress*, **30** (1), pp 66–81

2 DuPont
    – Dupont, G (1997) The dirty dozen errors in maintenance, in *Proceedings of the 11th Symposium on Human Factors in Aviation Maintenance*, FAA, Washington, DC
    – Van Opstal, D (2011) *Priorities for America's Preparedness: Best Practices from the Private Sector*, US Resilience Project, 2011, http://usresilienceproject.org/wp-content/uploads/2014/09/report-Priorities_for_Americas_Preparedness.pdf
    – DuPont (nd) 1805 Core Values, DuPont website, http://www2.dupont.com/Phoenix_Heritage/en_US/1805_detail.html
    – Atak, A and Kingma, S (2011) Safety culture in an aircraft maintenance organisation: A view from the inside, *Safety Science*, **49** (2), pp 268–78

3 Klein, JA (2009) Two centuries of process safety at DuPont, *Process Safety Progress*, **28** (2), pp 114–22

4 Shapira, P (1995) *The R&D Workers: Managing innovation in Britain, Germany, Japan, and the United States*, Greenwood Publishing, Westport, CT

5 Kalra, N, Hallegatte, S, Lempert, R *et al* (2014) *Agreeing on Robust Decisions: New processes for decision making under deep uncertainty*, World Bank Policy Research Working Paper 6906, Washington, DC

6 Making decisions with deep uncertainty:
    – Lempert, RJ (2003) *Shaping the Next One Hundred Years: New methods for quantitative, long-term policy analysis*. Rand Corporation, Santa Monica, CA
    – Kalra, N, Hallegatte, S, Lempert, R *et al* (2014) *Agreeing on Robust Decisions: New processes for decision making under deep uncertainty*, World Bank Policy Research Working Paper 6906, Washington, DC

7 Economic forecasting:
    – Burns, T (1986) The interpretation and use of economic predictions, *Proceedings of the Royal Society of London, A*, **407**, pp 103–25
    – Hendry, DF and Clements, MP (2003) Economic forecasting: some lessons from recent research, *Economic Modelling* **20** (2), pp 301–29

8 Craig, PP, Gadgil, A and Koomey, JG (2002) What can history teach us? A retrospective examination of long-term energy forecasts for the United States, *Annual Review of Energy and the Environment*, **27** (1), pp 83–118

9 Silver, N (2012) *The Signal and the Noise: Why so many predictions fail – but some don't*, Penguin Press, New York

10 Kolb, RA and Stekler, HO (1996) How well do analysts forecast interest rates? *Journal of Forecasting*, **15** (5), pp 385–94

11 QuakeCoRE is a new Centre of Research Excellence on Earthquake Resilience, established in 2016. You can find out more about QuakeCoRE and our work at: http://www.quakecore.nz/

12 Decision making in high-velocity environments:
   - Eisenhardt, KM (2008) Speed and strategic choice: how managers accelerate decision making, *California Management Review*, **50** (2), pp 102–16
   - Eisenhardt, KM (1999) Strategy as strategic decision making, *Sloan Management Review*, **40** (3), pp 65–72
   - Eisenhardt, KM (1989) Making fast strategic decisions in high-velocity environments, *Academy of Management Journal*, **32** (3), pp 543–76
   - Clark, K and Collins, C (2002) Strategic decision-making in high velocity environments: a theory revisited and a test, in *Creating Value: Winners in the new business environment*, ed MA Hitt, R Amit, CE Lucier *et al*, pp 213–39, Blackwell, Oxford

13 Rochlin, GI, La Porte, TR and Roberts, KH (1998) The self-designing high-reliability organization: aircraft carrier flight operations at sea, *Naval War College Review*, **51** (3), p 97

14 Fenwick, T, Seville, E and Brunsdon, D (2009) *Reducing the Impact of Organisational Silos on Resilience*, Resilient Organisations Research Report 2009/01, http://www.resorgs.org.nz/images/stories/pdfs/silos.pdf

Embedding it in the culture

08

The resilience of your organization depends on the quality of its leadership and culture, the networks and relationships your organization can draw on for support, and how your organization is strategically positioned to be change-ready. Through the course of this book I have introduced 13 indicators, identified through research, which you can use for diagnosing and improving your organization's resilience. Five of the 13 indicators are particularly important because of their influence. This book has covered each of these in depth: leadership, staff engagement, effective partnerships, situation awareness, and innovation and creativity. Get these five right, and your organization will not only be more resilient to adversity, it will also be a better business.

Resilience is not something that can be purchased off the shelf – it needs to be 'baked in' to your organization. Resilience needs to become part of your organization's ethos, culture and ways of operating. While at times this may feel like an unachievable goal, it is most definitely possible. Even the most dysfunctional of organizations can be transformed – but it requires deliberate and sustained effort. In this chapter, I outline three important elements for embedding resilience in your organization's culture: being intentional, keeping working at it, and capturing the opportunities.

Be intentional

Many of us have read books espousing the importance of good workplace culture for delivering high performance. And yet, *good* management practice isn't necessarily *common* management practice. Even though we know its importance, when the pressure comes on, our focus slips onto other things. SCIRT is an example of how being intentional about culture can deliver results.

Duncan Gibb had the task of forming a brand-new organization from scratch. He was the CEO and very first employee of SCIRT, an alliance set up to deliver $2 billion dollars' worth of infrastructure repairs and reconstruction. Duncan was working in the ultimate high-pressure environment – trying to rebuild a city following disaster. As an alliance, Duncan had to bring together local government and central government infrastructure owners, along with five major contracting firms, to repair and rebuild earthquake-damaged underground infrastructure across Christchurch.

From day one, Duncan took a very intentional approach to shaping SCIRT's culture. During every key decision he tried to keep one question at the front of his mind – will this move our organization towards or away from creating a culture where high performance will flourish?

Culture featured in decisions ranging from the office layout (with the bathrooms strategically placed at the centre of the building to encourage interaction between different groups) through to the naming of teams (the Red Team, the Blue Team etc), so that silos between staff seconded from different organizations would more quickly break down. The profit-share structure of the organization was designed so that the highest-performing teams would grow their share of the available work (encouraging competition), but all teams shared the financial penalties if one team didn't deliver (encouraging collaboration, with high-performing teams incentivized to support lower-performing teams to deliver). Key performance indicators included metrics relating to how groups contributed to the culture – with metrics relating to levels of collaboration, innovation and learning. Significant budget was invested in getting the culture right, with coaches brought in to help team dynamics. The result was an organization with a can-do culture. Staff were encouraged to lead, take initiative and be proactive.

We know that creating the right environment is vital for an organization to deliver success. What SCIRT demonstrates is that an organization's culture doesn't have to emerge by chance – it can be guided and influenced by the values and behaviours that the organization rewards.

If you want to create resilience within your organization, you need to do it with intention:

1 Sit down with your team and work out your organization's current resilience strengths and weaknesses. Use one of the tools suggested in the initiatives chapter as a starting point.

2 Identify some priorities. You can't fix everything at once. Select two or three areas you are going to work on first.

3 Pull together a diverse team to work on this important mission. With this team, develop a plan for how you are going to make improvements.

4 Implement your plan with discipline. Don't let this be a low-priority initiative – project-manage it as if it were for a client.

5 Track your progress. Report to the team on how things are progressing. Review and adjust your plan as required. Create SMART goals that are specific, measureable, assignable, realistic and time related.

6 Once the project is complete, celebrate its success and identify the next challenge you are going to tackle.

Don't just hope that your organization is going to be resilient – make it so. To paraphrase Duncan, hope is not a method – you need to be intentional. Why leave something so important to chance?

Keep working at it

Making your organization more resilient won't be achieved overnight. Pace your efforts. If you push through change too quickly within your organization, you will probably face resistance. Create a two- or three-year programme of work so that you can stage your resilience journey. Start with the low-hanging fruit (some of the smaller things that you think will be easiest to accomplish). That way, you will achieve some early wins. You can then work your way up to addressing the more challenging issues once you have created a sense of momentum and accomplishment.

Remember to bring others along with you on this journey. One of the best ways to do this is to align your resilience programme so that it helps others meet *their* key targets. For example, if your HR team is working on a particular project that has some resilience benefits, throw your efforts in behind its project to make it as successful as it can be. Remember that one of the golden rules of reciprocity is that you need to give to receive. Some people within your organization may feel threatened by all this talk of resilience – fearing that it is somehow detracting from their area of work. Aligning your resilience efforts so that it helps them to deliver on their organizational goals will earn you supporters for the future.

Make sure that you regularly review, re-orientate and re-energize your resilience programme so that it doesn't just fade away over time. Unfortunately, resilience isn't like a pot of gold. You can't stockpile it to pull out in times of emergency. As my colleague John Vargo likes to say, resilience is more like fitness. You need to keep working at it; otherwise it will quickly erode.

Capture the opportunities

After reading this book, you will be more aware of the need for your organization to be ready for change and adversity. But be prepared for others to be less open to the idea. When you talk with people about the imperative to become more resilient, don't just focus on the need to prepare for major disasters. Although disasters do happen and are happening all the time around the world, it is human nature to not really believe they are going to happen to us.

A better use of your energies is to make the case for resilience by demonstrating its benefits in everyday life. Resilience will ensure that your organization is alert to changes, and has the mindset and agility to respond. Opportunity abounds – but only if your organization has the capability and foresight to capture it. Rather than seeing resilience as another form of insurance, see it as an investment in making your organization more future-ready. It will enable your organization to thrive, irrespective of what the future may hold.

Summary

Key take-outs from this chapter:

- Even the least resilient of organizations can be transformed – but it requires deliberate and sustained effort.
- To create resilience within your organization, you need to do it with intention. Identify your priority areas of focus, develop a plan and deliver on that plan with the same discipline you would use to deliver an important client project.
- Set yourself up for success. Start with smaller things to address and work your way up to the more complex and challenging issues.
- Bring others along with you on the journey. Align your resilience programme with other organizational goals and objectives.
- Resilience is much more than being prepared for disasters – it is about ensuring that your organization is ready for any future.

Implementing resilience initiatives

09

In this final chapter, I provide practical ideas for how you can improve the resilience of your organization. These ideas are grouped according to the concepts presented in each chapter of this book. At the end of each chapter, I gave an indication of the most relevant initiatives – but there are many cross-overs, so don't feel constrained by that classification. If you think there is a way to you can tweak an idea to better suit your purposes, by all means do so.

Over the years, our Resilient Organisations team[1] has been collating ideas on different ways to improve an organization's resilience. In particular, Charlotte Brown has been a great contributor to this list. With so many different types of organization, all doing different things and operating in different contexts, there are few cookie-cutter resilience solutions that will work for every organization, every time. But within the following list, there are bound to be at least a handful of ideas that you can tailor to be perfect for your organization. Have a read, create yourself a shortlist of initiatives to try and then get started.

Initiate the resilience conversation

If you are the lone voice (or just a small team of voices) within your organization trying to get focus on resilience, here are some ideas for getting the conversation started:

1 **Get someone in to tell their story**: Sometimes people just can't or won't hear what you are saying. So rather than repeating yourself again

and again, have someone else be the messenger. Invite a really good speaker to come and present to your organization. Do you know an organization in your industry or local area that has recently been through some kind of crisis? Invite someone from that organization to come and share their experiences of what really helped, and what they wished they had had in place to help them through. To get people to engage with the concept of resilience, you need to capture both hearts and minds, so make the story personal. Ask the presenter to reflect on their personal experience of the crisis – how it affected them, what challenges and choices they faced, and their personal learnings from the event. Match the presenter to the audience. If it is your senior management team you want to influence, get someone at senior management level to come and talk with them. If it is your board that you want to influence, have a board member come to speak. Once people can imagine for themselves how your organization's non-resilience might impact on them personally, they often become receptive to learning more.

2 **Take advantage of burning platforms**: 'What if' scenarios are most powerful if people can see that they really can, and do, affect organizations in the real world. Next time there is a crisis in the news or affecting an organization in your industry, use that as a prompt to get people to reflect on how your organization would be affected in a similar situation. For example, if a local business has just had a major fire, use that as a trigger to think about your major vulnerabilities to a fire. How good are your organization's housekeeping practices? Are fire suppression systems regularly maintained? What cover would your insurance policies provide? How would you finance the recovery? How long do you think it might take to fix the damage and restore operations? Identify just a few issues that you think are priority areas and focus on these.

3 **Use a little peer pressure**: There is nothing like thinking that 'everyone else is doing it' to pique people's interest to find out more. Find ways to subtly raise the profile of what other organizations are doing to improve their resilience. Team up with others in your industry to compile a set of local case study examples that you can draw on the next time you talk about resilience.

4 **Let it be their idea**: While you, personally, want recognition for all the hard work you have been putting into improving your organization's resilience, the greater goal is to make your organization more resilient. Even though you may already know the best ways to improve your

organization's resilience, don't try to railroad things through. Slow down so that people can join you on this journey. People will often throw their efforts behind an initiative if they feel they have had real input into it. Find opportunities for others to come up with their own ideas and initiatives.

5 **Don't call it Resilience**: If you have a 'fad'-wary organization, and people think resilience is just another fad, think about how you frame resilience. Consider how the attributes discussed in this book link to your organization's existing objectives. Does your organization pride itself on its creativity? Great, sell crisis planning as a way to improve creativity. Or perhaps your organization is all about the bottom line: sell staff engagement initiatives based on their ability to improve productivity. Rather than thinking of resilience as yet another business objective or KPI, think about how you can align resilience with your organization's existing priorities.

6 **Use the Resilience HealthCheck to generate discussion and reflection**: The Australian Resilience Expert Advisory Group (REAG) has designed a neat little tool, which is freely available, to stimulate teams to collectively reflect on and discuss their organization's resilience strengths and weaknesses. The HealthCheck uses the same 13 indicators of resilience described in this book, and is designed to facilitate an 'aha' moment of insight into the importance of resilience. It is best used in a workshop format, and the value is in the discussion that the scores generate, not the scores themselves. Take a look at the HealthCheck: http://www.organisationalresilience.gov.au/HealthCheck/Pages/default.aspx[2]

Resilience benchmarking – comparisons within and between organizations

There is nothing like being able to compare an organization against its peers to stimulate interest and motivation. These initiatives show how collaborative resilience projects – involving multiple departments within an organization, or across a group of different organizations – can help inject a sense of purpose into your resilience programme:

7 **Test the waters using the Resilience Thumbprint**: Before launching a major benchmarking exercise, start with the simple first. Take the

Resilience Thumbprint survey yourself (Chapter 1, page 20). There is also a free online version of this tool that will provide you with a snapshot of how you perceive the resilience strengths and weaknesses of your organization: http://resorgs.resilientbusiness.co.nz/[3] The Resilience Thumbprint uses a cut-down set of questions drawn from the Benchmark Resilience Tool (see below), and takes only a few minutes to complete. The Resilience Thumbprint is designed to whet your appetite for exploring your organization's resilience profile further. Note that the Resilience Thumbprint captures only *one* perspective on your organization's resilience – yours. For a more complete picture, use the Benchmark Resilience Tool below.

8 **Benchmark the resilience of your organization**: The Benchmark Resilience Tool (BRT) is an online survey tool that allows you to evaluate the resilience of your organization and benchmark it against other organizations. It helps identify your organization's resilience strengths and weaknesses and track your progress over time. The BRT has been developed and tested by Resilient Organisations through a decade of research into what makes some organizations rise to the challenges presented by crisis, while others fail. It is based around the 13 indicators of resilience, relating to an organization's leadership and culture, networks and relationships, and change readiness. The tool involves two surveys – the first to be completed by the CEO or other senior manager, and the second to be completed by as many individuals within the organization as possible (or a sufficiently large sample in the case of very large organizations). These perspectives are combined to provide a comprehensive view of the organization's resilience qualities. Results are collated and analysed to provide a measure of how your organization is tracking against each of the 13 indicators. Results can be contrasted between different departments or geographic locations within your organization, to identify pockets of best practice that can be shared. For more information on the BRT, see: http://www.resorgs.org.nz/benchmark-resilience-tool.html[4]

9 **Partner with other organizations to benchmark and improve resilience together**: There are a number of ways that you can come together with other organizations to collectively improve resilience. Organizations have different inherent strengths – so getting together is a great way to leverage off each other's strengths. For example, our team has worked with five water utility companies in Australia to benchmark and compare their resilience. [5] The utilities all had different resilience strengths, highlighting

opportunities for sharing of ideas and best practices across the companies. In another project, we worked with a regional cluster of 18 critical infrastructure providers,[6] to evaluate each organization's resilience individually (using the BRT discussed above), and then looked across the 18 organizations to identify areas of common strength and weakness. The organizations then worked together on a joint initiative to help them all improve a common weakness (in their case – stress-testing plans). The important feature of these projects was that they initiated conversations and reflections *between* organizations about how their organization's structure, operations and culture were all influencing resilience. You could set up similar initiatives with organizations in your area. Start by undertaking a review of each organization's resilience strengths and weaknesses, to provide a baseline to work from (you could use any of the tools described above). Then, together, select a few areas to focus on. These could be areas of shared weakness, or areas where one organization has a particular strength and could therefore help the others to improve. Another approach could be to do a resilience review of each other's organization (eg by interviewing staff to identify areas where improvements are needed), and then comparing results. Yet another option could be to evaluate each other's crisis exercises, providing an external evaluation of areas for improvement. Sharing ideas between organizations can be a great and cost-effective way to move your resilience programme forward. You will get even more learning and new ideas if you partner with organizations from sectors different from yours.

10 **Audit resilience capabilities:** Don't just audit the things that are easy to audit (such as whether your organization has a plan and how often it is tested). This year, why not focus your audit programme on how effectively you are improving your organization's resilience capabilities? Is there a defined action plan for addressing identified resilience weaknesses? How well are those plans being implemented? Are there tangible improvements being observed?

Develop crisis leadership capability

Few of us regularly practise dealing with situations that are well beyond our comfort zone, involve extreme levels of uncertainty and compressed time-frames, and put us under considerable emotional stress. It takes practice to become good at working, and leading, in these environments:

11 Self-evaluate and actively improve your own leadership skills: Leadership needs to come from all levels of the organization – so that means you! Do not assume that you are a good leader. Be bold. Ask an intermediary to go out and ask what people think of you as a leader. You might be surprised that the leadership style you think you are delivering isn't the style being received. Asking a neutral person to gather views from staff will give you a more honest appraisal of the areas you need to work on. Try not to let your ego get in the way. Don't be defensive if there are more weaknesses identified than you were expecting. See the information in the spirit it was given – to help you become an even better leader for the benefit of everyone. Once you have identified some areas to work on, be prepared to take action to moderate those weaknesses. There are many resources available for ideas on how to improve your leadership – ranging from books, through TED talks and getting a leadership coach, to going on a training course. You can also download a copy of our free booklet *Chaos to Teamwork: A leader's role in crisis*: http://www.resorgs.org.nz/chaos-to-teamwork.html[7]

12 Exercise strategic dilemmas: Many organizations invest significant effort in exercising (which is just another name for practising and testing) their response to simulated crises. All too often, however, these exercises are designed to test the organization's *operational* response to a crisis. The most senior people in the organization don't always participate, losing a significant opportunity to hone their crisis leadership skills. If you want to build crisis leadership capabilities within your organization, you need to design crisis exercises to include *strategic* dilemmas. For example, practise managing bad publicity, a quality issue, strike action, or the rapid emergence of an aggressive competitor. Ensure that there are no simple solutions, so the team has to debate the pros and cons of alternative responses. Involve leadership coaches to work alongside key people during these exercises to explore the implications of different leadership responses.

13 Capture both hearts and minds: Having trouble getting the leaders in your organization to really engage with crisis preparedness? For one reason or another, senior executives always seem to have other, more pressing priorities. In one organization I worked with, we designed a crisis exercise to change that. The exercise involved an active shooter (ie someone with a gun) roaming their large campus of buildings. Within minutes of the exercise starting, the executives were told there were three media helicopters flying overtop, that the offenders had set up video cameras streaming live feeds onto the internet, and that the phone-lines were jammed with incoming calls as news of the attacks spread. They had thousands of people on the premises and few means of communication to tell them what to do. After several hours of working through the scenario, the exercise was rounded out with two very moving talks from people who had experienced active shooting incidents at work. These talks really brought home the importance of managing a crisis well. That exercise became a turning point. Never again did the executive team think emergency management was just the remit of security. From that day forward, it was the leadership team who were asking when their next exercise would be. Could a similar approach work for your organization?

14 **Build the leadership skills of junior and middle leaders**: Given that good leadership is needed at all levels of your organization, don't just focus on improving the leadership of your most senior staff. Focus on growing crisis leadership throughout your organization. To do this in a cost-effective way, consider creating a leadership mentoring scheme. This will improve the leadership skills of both the mentor and the person they are mentoring, providing a prompt for both to consciously reflect on their leadership styles. You could also partner with another organization to swap mentors, injecting fresh perspectives into your organization and helping to develop a range of leaders and leadership styles.

15 **Empower your staff to lead during a crisis**: Ensure that your business continuity or crisis plan includes decision-making delegations. If Mary is not available, Sue will make the decision. Or, in X situation, Bob has authority to do A, B and C. Make sure these delegations are flexible (for example, by position not by person), because you can never be sure who will and who won't be available during a crisis. Devolve as many decisions as possible. Ask yourself what actually needs to be decided at an organizational level and what can be handled at a departmental or individual level. Review all business-as-usual delegations and decide what can be changed in a crisis. For example, is there a spending limit than can be increased in emergencies to allow staff to buy emergency supplies without getting permission? Empower your staff to make decisions and lead in a crisis.

16 **Build a crisis leadership team**: Teams take time and practice to settle down and work well together. US National Transportation Safety Board incident data show that airline incidents are significantly more likely on the first day a crew fly together.[8] Given this, you don't want to bring

your crisis management team together for the first time in the midst of a crisis. Think about who should be in your crisis team. Who would be good to work with in a crisis? Ensure that you have some diversity, as it will improve innovation and decision making and will avoid tunnel vision – where an immediate crisis is solved only to miss, or even aggravate, the larger looming crisis. Consider complementary skills and backgrounds, including: gender, age, technical skills, background, and thinking styles. Even if you are a very small organization, remember that two heads are better than one. You will make better and more confident decisions if you have a trusted group of people with whom to work through the situation.

Build staff engagement

Do your staff feel invested in your organization? For staff to be effective in a crisis, particularly when they have personal challenges to deal with, they have to *want* to come to work. Do your staff feel this way? If not, ask staff why. Listen to their responses and act on them. Be intentional about creating a work environment that delivers resilience – don't leave it to chance:

17 **Run a staff engagement survey**: Staff who are engaged in their work are likely to be there to help when the chips are down. Give staff a chance to provide feedback honestly, perhaps through a regular staff engagement survey. And make sure you listen and act on the feedback. If you haven't run a staff engagement survey before, Survey Monkey and the Society for Human Resource Management Foundation have partnered to provide resources that will help. These include standard questions, templates for analysing results, and benchmarking data to see how your organization's results compare. See https://www.surveymonkey. com/mp/employee-engagement-survey/[9]

18 **Have dual job descriptions for staff**: Make sure your staff are clear about their roles in a crisis situation. One way to do this is by adding a 'during adversity' section to their job description. This is a great way to embed the concept that everyone has a role to play in times of crisis. Every time you run a crisis exercise, get people to adopt their 'during adversity' role. Not only does this ensure that everyone knows what their role will be, but it also challenges the organization to think deeply about how best to make use of all the people resources it has available.

19 **Make work a place that staff want to come to**: Organize social events to help build friendships across your organization. It doesn't have to be expensive – sponsor a work team in the 'social' grade of a local sports competition, organize a catered morning tea, some after-work drinks or a bowling night. Different people will have different interests, so ensure you have a range of events to draw them in.

20 **Support the families of your staff**: Show staff that your organization knows how important their families are to them. In times of crisis, helping to support families will mean staff have one less thing to worry about and can focus on the task at hand. Make a holiday home available for staff, hold staff and family picnics, provide staff with a cleaning or laundry service. Better yet, ask your staff what their families need in a crisis.

21 **Play the Wellbeing Game**: If your people are not finding the right balance in their lives, they aren't likely to be productive for you at work. The Mental Health Foundation of New Zealand has developed the Wellbeing Game, which can be used within organizations to help staff focus on the Five Ways to Wellbeing: be active, take notice, connect, give, and keep learning. You can read more about the Wellbeing Game and how to use it in your workplace at: http://thewellbeinggame.org.nz/home/how[10]

22 **Review how well your organization is supporting employee resilience**: The Employee Resilience Tool will help you to understand how your organization is impacting the resilience of your employees. Rather than focusing on the personal resilience of individual staff members, this tool provides a diagnostic for how well your organization's culture promotes and supports the resilience of staff. You can find the latest version of the Employee Resilience Tool here: http://www.resorgs.org.nz/Resources/employee-resilience-tool.html[11] If you are using the tool to survey your staff, ensure that they can answer anonymously and let them know that their responses reflect on the organization, not on them personally. When analysing the results, look for overall patterns rather than individual responses. You can also use this tool as a prompt to think about how you yourself are as an employee and if there are ways you could improve your own resilience at work. Now, put your manager's hat on. Look at the questions again. Which aspects do your staff struggle with most? How might you be able to shift that?

23 **Engage staff in everyday business decisions and challenges**: Staff will feel more invested in your organization if they are involved in everyday decisions and challenges. And, what's more, you will get better

and more creative solutions to problems. In a crisis situation, it is very likely that you will be overwhelmed by the number and magnitude of decisions to be taken. You need to utilize the talents, knowledge and skills of your staff. This will have benefits in business-as-usual as well – staff will feel trusted and empowered to take charge of their work and will have an increased sense of ownership in the business. Start today. Think of a work problem you have been trying to solve. Get together two or three staff members with whom to discuss the problem. Aim to do this at least once a week.

Develop effective partnerships

Think about everyone who is critical to your organization's operations – both during business-as-usual and during times of crisis: customers, clients, regulators, industry partners, competitors, suppliers and your suppliers' suppliers. Make an effort to build good, respectful and trusted relationships with all these organizations:

24 **Establish mutual aid agreements**: Crises affect everyone. Team up with other organizations to see how you could help each other in times of trouble. This could be a pro bono or paid arrangement. Things to consider include: what resources each organization might have available to offer, what the process would be for requesting and providing assistance, how to integrate these resources into your operations (eg if their staff come to work alongside yours, how those teams will be managed, what liability issues need to be considered, how costs will be allocated and reimbursed). Unless yours is a response agency, where mutual aid agreements are an important aspect of fulfilling your organization's obligations, then as a first step you may find it better to focus on establishing the principles for offering and accepting mutual aid, rather than trying to nail everything down contractually. Too often, mutual aid arrangements never get made because of difficulties getting people to agree, in advance, on the specifics. But if the willingness is there, and the relationship is strong, it is amazing what can be achieved with a few simple phone calls during a crisis. Those conversations are much easier if some foundational work has been done in advance. When setting up mutual aid arrangements, it is important to fully understand

the other organization's risks and, as far as possible, make sure that you have as few common risks as possible (eg you aren't both likely to be flooded at the same time). Also consider who else may be relying on the same resources as you. If there is a major crisis, others may have greater priority than you, and the resources you thought you had access to may no longer be available.

25 **Make resilience a core focus of procurement**: Have your procurement team review how well your supply arrangements work from a resilience perspective. Consider adding 'resilience' as another criterion to the evaluation process for selecting suppliers. Also think about whether your procurement policies promote the forming of lasting and effective relationships. Resilience requires building social connections, not just transactional relationships. If you are constantly switching suppliers to get the lowest cost, this may have resilience implications. Add crisis arrangements to business-as-usual contracts. If your contractors and suppliers are vital to the continuity of your business, consider including crisis arrangements within normal contracts. (For example, what are the service delivery expectations during times of crisis? What if a critical component is in short supply – can you get priority service over other customers?) Internationally, there have been many advances in recent years on supply-chain management best practices to improve resilience. Increasingly, multinationals will require all suppliers to have business continuity plans in place, and they are becoming far more proactive in working with suppliers to collectively improve resilience. There is also growing recognition of the need to assess supply-chain vulnerabilities from a systems perspective, to identify the potential ripple effects of disruption throughout the supply web. As the Thailand floods example in Chapter 4 illustrates, the source of a disruption might not be your direct supplier – but from several steps along the supply chain.

26 **Organize social events with partners**: In times of crisis, it is only natural that the people you can most rely on are those with whom you get on well. Put effort into building friendships with the people you work with, so that they become the kind of person you could call on at 3 am to help. Start small. Get into the habit of asking people how their weekend was, or how their family is doing. On a larger scale, hold an annual social event, a barbeque or a game of bowls, with your key suppliers and customers.

27 **Help someone out**: Social capital is all about reciprocity. You need to give in order to receive. It is important to offer support and to say yes if

people ask for your help. Supporting another organization through times of crisis has benefits for both organizations. It will forge a stronger relationship between your organizations. It was also provide your team with valuable crisis experience and learnings.

Keep a finger on the pulse

How regularly does your organization engage with others in your business community, your industry and local community? The more people you know and interact with, the more information that is relevant to your business they will funnel your way:

28 Take the time to get to know people: To build your organization's situation awareness requires tapping your networks. Collectively, your staff have networks that go well beyond those of senior managers – but you won't know about many of these networks unless you know your staff well. Carve out time to interact with them. If your meetings generally have very full agendas, there is little chance for opportune connections to come up. Take some time to catch up with your staff over a coffee. At your next meeting, rather than just getting people to introduce themselves in the usual way, get them also to highlight three social groups they are connected with (eg they might be a coach for a soccer team, they might be a parent of a toddler, they might be in a local band, they might volunteer at the local homeless centre). You might just discover something that you never knew before.

29 Actively scan the horizon: Create a forum within your organization that actively looks for emerging threats and opportunities. This doesn't need to be a complex or costly process. You could create a horizon-scanning team that meets for a few hours each month. Task them with scanning for changes, both internally and externally, that could affect your organization. To gain insights on issues that could potentially affect your sector (but may not yet be on the horizon of anyone in your organization), consider tapping into an existing sector association or professional forum to collectively identify emerging trends. If your organization is operating in a highly competitive industry (where the last thing you want to do is share intelligence with your competitors), form a scanning team with others from your profession who might work in different sectors. Encourage staff to be on the lookout for latent risks and to share them with their manager. Make sure you have easy ways to communicate these ideas. Maybe run a competition with staff to identify things that could affect your organization, and ways to monitor them. One of our team, Charlotte Brown, recalls as a new graduate being tasked by her manager to read the newspaper every morning to see if there was anything relevant to their organization. This is a great, simple idea for getting staff to be more aware of where your organization sits in the world. When people do bring issues to your attention, be sure to recognize it.

30 **Get people thinking beyond tomorrow**: To get people thinking about future trends and disruptive technologies, each month ask a different member of your team to pick a topic (eg the implications of an ageing workforce, the emergence of the internet-of-things, the 2015 Paris Agreement on Climate Change, driverless cars...) and give a 10-minute presentation on the potential implications of this shift for your organization. The idea is not to expect people to be able to forecast what will or won't occur, but to develop a mindset within your team to be curious and explore alternative futures for how a situation could unfold over time.

31 **Continually review your business model**: Why might people stop buying from you? What are your competitors doing? What is the next big shift in your market? Just because your business model was fit for purpose a few years ago, doesn't mean it will remain so. It is important to take a fresh look at your business regularly and to ensure that it is future-ready. Run a customer survey to find out what your customers are doing and what they think.

Become a learning organization

How often do your staff come up with an idea for improvement? How often have these ideas been implemented? Find ways to keep ideas flowing. You will need this creativity in harder times:

32 **Co-create solutions**: If there is a problem, make sure those involved in the problem are involved in the solution, too. Take the time to really understand why the problem has emerged in the first place. Draw together 'challenge teams' with members from across your organization. Working together to find solutions to specific problems helps to break down a 'them and us' mentality, where one part of the organization is

perceived to be the cause of all the problems. Don't wait for a major crisis before forming your challenge teams – bring them together for smaller issues so that they can learn to work well together.

33 **Get people thinking outside the box**: As humans, we can stifle our creative thoughts by the bounds of what we think is possible. Yet the best ideas are often outside this box. Inspire and encourage creative thinking – where any idea is a good idea. Hold a monthly 'back of the envelope' innovation challenge. Give your staff a real or hypothetical problem to solve and get them to post their ideas on the staff notice board. Acknowledge and reward the best ideas. Keep it simple and keep it fun, and you will soon get people joining in. We run an internal competition with our research team whenever we need a name for our new booklets. The best suggestion wins a dinner voucher. For the price of a meal we get showered with great name suggestions (eg 'Shut Happens' and 'Staffed or Stuffed'), everyone has a bit of fun, and the broader team gets to know about our latest offering to come out.

34 **Gather in more and better ideas**: One of my colleagues, Nilakant, taught me a great technique which I have found works in almost any context. It is a form of brainstorming, but with some structure put around it. Get a group together and explain the issue that you need resolving (eg how to break down silo mentality between two departments, or how to overcome your dependence on an unreliable supplier). Tell them there are no constraints – money is not a problem. Get them to write down, on their own, as many different ways they can think of for how this issue could be resolved. Give them 5–7 minutes to do this. Then go round the group and ask them to read out their full list (if time is short or the group is large, ask them just to give their best three or five ideas). The facilitator should write down the ideas on flipchart paper (or any technology – just so long as the group can see it). The ideas should be written as a numbered list –1, 2, 3,…. If people have the same idea as one that has already been written on the list, they should still read it out, but it won't be added to the written list. Once all the ideas are on the list, tell the group you want them to brainstorm again, but this time they are not allowed to repeat any of the ideas already on the list. Again, give people 5–7 minutes on their own to think up potential solutions, and then once more go around the group and add people's ideas to the growing list of potential solutions. You can repeat this cycle again if time allows. What you will find is that the number of ideas gets fewer with each iteration, but their creativity and quality increase markedly. People get pushed beyond thinking about

the 'usual' solutions, to come up with really new and different ways to address the challenge. It is not unusual to come up with between 50 and 100 great ideas for how an issue could be resolved.

35 **Draw in fresh perspectives**: The Australian water sector has come up with a simple yet highly effective technique for injecting fresh thinking during the pressure of an unfolding crisis – it activates a national phone link-up. With crisis managers from water companies right around the country, the organization in crisis can ask for input on problems or issues it is currently dealing with. The people on the call are fresh – their organization isn't in crisis, so they aren't sleep deprived or feeling under pressure. They are able to think clearly and bring a wealth of diverse experience and expertise to the table. As the people on the call are from outside the organization, they are able to ask questions that otherwise wouldn't be raised – often coming up with completely new perspectives and ideas on how the crisis could be managed. These national phone link-ups have been used successfully during crisis exercises, and a number of national and international crises, including the Brisbane floods, the Victoria bushfires and the Christchurch earthquakes. Could you try something similar for your organization?

36 **Go gravity-free**: Sometimes we get so hung up on how a problem can't be solved that we become less open to finding ways it *can* be solved. So, get your team out of a rut by mixing things up a little. Change venue and meet them off-site for a brainstorming session. Bring different people together – great ideas can come from diverse perspectives. Create teams with people of different ages, genders and from different departments – give them a challenge to work through together. Task them with coming up with the most innovative (and effective) solution possible.

37 **Develop problem solvers in your team**: Cultivate your team's ability to come up with their own solutions before seeking input from supervisors or managers. Independent problem-solving skills are vital in a crisis and will also enhance your day-to-day operations. Encourage staff to discuss problems over morning tea with colleagues. Investigate new techniques to add to your problem-solving toolkit. For example, the Design School at Stanford provides some great advice on how to use design thinking principles for problem solving. It even offers a free bootcamp design course which you could try with your team: http://dschool.stanford.edu/use-our-methods/[12]

38 **Is yours a learning organization?** Discover the extent to which your organization really does have all the required building blocks to become a

learning organization: a supportive environment, concrete learning processes and practices, and leadership that reinforces learning. Use the free, online diagnostic Organizational Learning tool: http://los.hbs.edu[13]

39 Be intentional about learning lessons: Take a leaf out of the US Army's book and get serious about not just identifying lessons, but actually learning them. Implement an After Action Review (AAR) process within your organization. A quick internet search will yield lots of resources for helping you to do this. One I particularly like is an article called 'Learning from action: imbedding more learning into the performance fast enough to make a difference'.[14] As the authors eloquently describe it, the AAR process is a way for a team to reflect on and learn while it is performing. You do not wait until the patient is dead to figure out what went wrong. The objective is to learn as you perform – to understand why interim objectives are not being met, what lessons can be learnt, and to drive those lessons back into the performance process. It works best if done immediately and is focused on just a few critical issues rather than being a full debrief. It needs to be structured, include everyone and, most importantly, lead back to action quickly. Remember that a lesson is not learnt unless something changes.

Plan for the unexpected

Murphy's law: *if it can go wrong it will go wrong*. So rather than being surprised when the unexpected occurs, be proactive and prepare for it:

40 Get better at managing risk: Get your staff together and do a really thorough risk identification exercise. Ask your team: what could affect us? Think big, small, internal, external, people, processes, premises, technology. And acknowledge the potential for the totally unforeseen risk that could be around the corner. Involve key suppliers or customers in this exercise, too, to find out what risks they are facing. Also keep an eye on internal operations – risks can come from inside your organization. Ensure that you have processes for identifying and escalating emerging issues. It could be something as small as a disagreement between two staff members, or a tardy supplier. Remember that there are many different types of risk. Some might be sudden (like an earthquake), while others could be gradual (such as a drought, or changes to consumer behaviour). Getting better at managing risk is an important discipline for any organization, as it helps to reduce the number of crises your organization will face. Team risk management with business continuity planning so that you have ways of keeping your business going if a risk does come to fruition. There are many great resources available that describe how to establish good risk management and business continuity practices within an organization. A good starting place would be the International Standards on Risk Management (ISO 31000) and Business Continuity Management (ISO 22301).[15] If you are just starting out, don't be daunted. Start with the simple and gradually improve over time. Brainstorm possible risks and their effects with your team; then get them to identify the three most disruptive effects and concentrate on developing strategies to manage those. If you feel that your organization already has good risk and business continuity management practices, stress-test how well your systems really are working. Think of the last five 'surprises' your organization experienced – did these feature on your risk register? Were they being adequately managed – and if not, why not? Did your alternative continuity arrangements work as expected? Few management systems will catch everything – but doing a cross-check to diagnose areas of weakness is a good starting place for making it even better.

41 **Learn from the past**: One of the best opportunities to learn about your organization's resilience is to review how well your organization has coped with past adversity. What worked well and what didn't? What knowledge do you need to capture and transmit to the next generation that may face a similar crisis? Since crises may not happen to your organization every day, near-misses provide a rich opportunity to learn. Consider ways to encourage people to report near-misses so that they are not swept under the carpet, but are instead used as learning opportunities. Ask your staff what might deter them from reporting an incident. You may discover that the amount of paperwork they are required to fill out is enough to put anyone off reporting anything in your organization. Foster a no-blame culture and reward those that do report. Draw a name out of the hat each month for a small reward (eg a dinner out) from all the incident reports you have received. Once you have incidents being reported, analyse this data to identify trends and what changes are needed. Be sure to share this information with staff so that they can see how the information they report is being put to good use.

42 **Develop plans with your team**: A bit of planning goes a long way. Even if your organization is starting from a very low level, a lot can be achieved in just a few years to build capability for dealing with crisis

events. But it does require the hard work and collaboration of a team of champions who believe in the cause, including support from senior managers. The process of planning is important. It helps to train you and your staff to think about potential risks and to develop innovative problem-solving skills that will be invaluable when a crisis occurs. It may even help you avoid a crisis. Have a monthly lunchtime brainstorming session where you present a crisis scenario and get your team to work through the possible responses. Take these ideas and develop or update your emergency or business continuity plan. This process may well be more valuable than the plan itself.

43 Practise decision making without all the information: Often we want to build our staff's confidence in their ability to manage crises, so we create crisis exercise scenarios that are solvable. Be bold and simulate reality – give your staff, and delegated decision makers, practice at making decisions without all the necessary information. For example, a number of your customers have reported food poisoning after eating your product. There are no tests to confirm this. What do you do? Staff need practice to build their skills and confidence. Teach them to pause and look for parallels to other situations they may have dealt with before. If there aren't any, they need to become confident in making decisions without all of the facts – and expect to have to some cleaning-up afterwards. Most importantly, though, they need to learn to make a decision and move on. As your crisis scenarios increase in complexity, your staff may find themselves facing strategic dilemmas where there is no obvious 'right' course of action – each has its downside. To help them work through these strategic choices, have staff print out a copy of your organization's core values and stick it on the wall above their desk. This provides a valuable reference point to ensure they are focusing on the right things. Once they are practised at dealing with these sorts of challenge, up the ante a little. Form an adversary team and war-game your next scenario – so one team is trying to solve the problem, while the other team is trying to come up with all the reasons why that solution won't work. Run a crisis exercise that involves strategic decisions, but take out your key managers: they are snowed in at a remote mountain lodge (at a strategic planning meeting) while your organization faces a damaging industrial waste leak. Is anyone prepared to step up? If not, you need to implement decision delegation and train more staff in crisis decision making.

44 Practise 'activating' a crisis response: One of your best tools for managing an emerging crisis is getting the right people in a room together. How you get the right people together quickly is referred to as the activation process. Activation is really important – it needs to be well thought out and second nature to people. Think about how people will be notified of a situation emerging. Even though it may be hard to miss that an emergency is unfolding from where you are, never assume that everyone is aware of an incident. Have an activation checklist so that little 'thinking' is required for those first few steps in the response process. Have a pre-identified emergency operations centre (EOC) as a known gathering point so that there is no confusion over where to go to join the response effort. Use this EOC regularly for training and meetings so that you know in advance how the space works, and people become familiar with the environment.

45 **Print out the Quick Start Guides**: At the end of each chapter within this book is a Quick Start Guide. These can be used in the heat of a crisis, as a prompt to respond in a more resilient way. During a crisis, the last thing you want to do is to be hunting through the book to find those nuggets of information, so I have created a compendium of them, available for free download: http://resorgs.org.nz/resilience-quickstart-guides[16] I suggest you print these out and include them in your emergency plan, or, even better, create posters for sticking on the wall of your designated EOC.

46 **Regularly test your emergency plans**: Whether you have business continuity, emergency or crisis plans (or all of the above), you need to test them all the time. Run one large test every year. Also do four or five other small tests during the year. Make sure you involve everyone in the drills. No two crises are the same, but thinking and discussing the issues before a crisis hits enables your team to be better prepared for the uncertain, complex and novel situations you may face. Perhaps piggyback a stress-test onto a fire drill so that instead of a 10-minute fire drill, you take 15 or 20 minutes and check another backup system. While your staff are assembled outside, give them a scenario to plan for: 'they have to work from home for the rest of the week', 'your key supplier has stopped operating', 'a competitor has come up with a superior product' etc. If you work in a small organization, crisis exercises need not be hugely time consuming or expensive. Have a morning tea or Friday drinks and put some scenarios to your team. These can range from the simple (if you are a bakery, what do we do if we come in one morning and the oven does not work?) to the more complicated (what do we do if there is a fire in our building and everything inside is damaged?). Make

sure you consider people, premises, processes and technology. Talking through the issues and alternative options will quickly help to frame the key priorities. Your staff will have ideas, access to other networks or resources, and they need to be ready to roll these out in the event of a crisis. Remember, you or other senior staff may not be there. Rather than focusing on the source of the disruption (eg natural disasters or power cuts), plan for how to manage consequences. For example: your building is inaccessible, half of your staff are unavailable, or e-mail is not working. You will get a broader range of ideas than when using an event-based scenario. Your staff will also learn to recognize that the plans they are testing could relate to a number of different situations. Remember that the point of running crisis scenarios is not to come up with right or wrong answers, but to explore the key vulnerabilities of your business and just what your options may be. Team crisis planning is a great way to get staff involved in the organization, and it grows their sense of ownership and loyalty – but this may take time to develop. Recognize emergency preparedness as professional development and properly train your staff to do the things you will expect of them. Make it fun and keep repeating it.

47 Prepare for recovery, not just response: So often we focus on what we will do within the first few hours of a crisis, but forget to prepare ourselves (both mentally and practically) for the recovery period that comes after. Recovery can be a long and hard journey. To get you thinking about what might be required, download our free booklet *First Aid for Your Business: In the midst of crisis?* from http://www.resorgs. org.nz/first-aid-business.html[17]

48 Run exercises with other organizations: Get together with a key business partner – a supplier, the local authority, a customer or even a competitor – and run through some crisis scenarios. Run scenarios that will affect one or both of you, and see how you can work together to meet everyone's needs. You will undoubtedly get a broader range of ideas than if you work alone. Remember that, in the heat of the moment, it is not the fine-print of contract wording that counts, but good personal relationships.

49 Socialize your plans: The reason why many business continuity and emergency management plans are ineffective is that they are developed by a separate team or by consultants tasked with the role. The plan then sits on a shelf gathering dust for the next few years, being pulled out once a year (if at all) to be 'tested'. The problem with such an approach is that in a crisis, few organizations actually reach for the plan off the shelf – they instead respond instinctively. The plan isn't implemented because people had 'forgotten' that it existed, or people didn't connect the dots and see how it was relevant, or they discover that the plan is out of date because a new system or process had been implemented. Run a review to see who in your organization is actually familiar with all the plans you have made. If you discover gaps, look for ways to better embed your plans into your organization's day-to-day operating reality. Perhaps the plan isn't a document filed away. Could you have it as a folder sitting on everyone's computer desktop? Maybe it is front and centre on your organization's intranet site? Make the plan visible and accessible, and give people reason to visit it regularly. You could also get new employees to review the plan as part of their induction, so everyone knows that crisis preparedness is part of their core role.

50 Map your staff vulnerabilities: If you want your staff to be there for your organization in times of crisis, you also need to support staff when they are in crisis. Get your staff to identify the potential challenges they may face in an emergency (childcare, transportation, community responsibilities). Include these in your crisis planning. Do what you can to enable your most critical staff to work – providing childcare or family support services if required. Sometimes it is the little things that make a big difference, such as food. Providing catering not only helps staff feel valued, but also provides a hub for interaction. Your planning also needs to recognize that people can't work long hours indefinitely. Just five consecutive nights of reduced sleep reduces people's cognitive performance to the equivalent of 48 hours straight without sleep.[18] Make sure you give people downtime so that they can work at their best. If the situation requires staff not to come to work, don't just forget about them. Keeping people away from work for too long can create a sense of disengagement, so it is important to counter this with personal communications from their manager or team leader so that people feel connected. Ensure that your team leaders know this is an important task for them. Also remember that as life for the majority gets back to normal, paradoxically, it gets harder for those who cannot yet get back to normal. Remain sensitive to people's circumstances. Recovery is a long haul, and the worst effects may be delayed. For more on how to look after your staff during an extended crisis, download a copy of our free booklet *Staffed or Stuffed*: http://www.resorgs.org.nz/staffed-or-stuffed.html[19]

51 Ensure you have funds set aside for a 'rainy day': Cash-flow issues can be a killer for any organization, so think carefully about what finances your organization might need to get through the immediate aftermath of a crisis. Remember, there can be significant delays before any insurance or grant payments may be available.

52 **Get the most out of your insurance**: Insurance is an important source of funds for many organizations following a crisis – but it is only useful if the policy delivers what you need, when you need it. For tips on how to select the right insurance policy, how to prepare to use your policy and how to claim on your insurance policy, download our free booklet *Cover Your Assets*: http://www.resorgs.org.nz/cover-your-assets.html[20] Insurance claims can be very complex and time consuming to manage – just at the time when your business needs you most. Many policies will cover the costs of a professional claims preparer to support your organization. In the event of a claim, you will want the best team on your side, so get some recommendations of good claims preparers in advance that you might wish to use.

53 **Make sure you can contact people**: You need to be able to contact your staff when a crisis happens – to check they are OK, coordinate, and keep your business running. Remember that you need to have contact information for a range of circumstances. What if the mobile phone network is down or if people's mobile phones are left in evacuated buildings? You also need to consider emergency contacts – whom to contact if a staff member is hurt at work. Include alternative phone numbers and methods for reaching people (e-mails, home addresses and phone numbers) with your contact information. Being able to contact each other is a key first step to beginning recovery from any major crisis. If your organization is large, consider ways your staff can let you know they are OK, so you can then focus your efforts on contacting those you haven't heard from yet (for example, using reverse phone trees or other mechanisms). Once your staff contact lists are up to date, you need to consider who else you might need to connect with in an emergency. Think about who your key suppliers and customers are. Communication with both suppliers and customers may help to preserve those relationships through the period of disruption. Also, consider whom you might need to contact in an emergency – bankers, insurers, lawyers, accountants?

54 **Prepare key communications messages in advance**: During a crisis you need to communicate, communicate, communicate. As part of your planning process, think about what sorts of key messages you might need to get out quickly. Pre-script these so they just need a quick review

before sending out during the heat of a crisis. Communications messages need to be consistent and yet tailored to the particular audience. Develop a crisis communications plan – setting out all the key stakeholders and who will be communicating with each of them, so no one is missed out.

Adapting ways of operating

If you can 'bake in' to your organization a natural ability to flex and evolve, it has a significant capacity to adapt to changing situations:

55 **Use crisis response capabilities to deal with everyday business challenges**: Sometimes crises aren't of the 'big-bang' variety, but can be more of a slow burn or chronic stress. Gradual decline of market-share or eroding customer satisfaction can result in just as severe a crisis as the failure of an IT system or a fire. These kinds of crisis, however, can be challenging to manage, because they are difficult to recognize and it can be difficult to mobilize the organization to respond. Rather like the frog in a pot of heating water, it can take so long for an organization to react that there are few response options left by the time the situation is recognized for what it is. This is why it is very important for an organization to develop sensors for identifying danger signals. Often organizations will deal with slow-burn crises using business-as-usual responses. This misses the opportunity to draw on the very strengths that an organization's crisis response mechanisms can bring to the table – the drawing together of cross-organization response teams, creating a sense of urgency for dealing with the problem, and encouraging people to think outside their 'normal' ways of working and to be innovative and creative in finding alternative solutions. Next time you have a slow-burn crisis emerging, try using your crisis response arrangements.

56 **Develop good decision-making practices**: Get into the habit, during business-as-usual, of using decision-making techniques that will also serve you well during times of crisis. We all have a natural tendency to procrastinate when information is poor and stakes are high – so learn from successful organizations that operate in these types of environment every day.[21] High-velocity environments are characterized by high levels of uncertainty and rapid change. Organizations that do well in these

environments tend to have a highly functional leadership team, with particular decision-making styles. For example, many will consider multiple alternative courses of action in parallel. Considering options A, B and C together helps prevent becoming 'locked on' to a particular strategy, continuing to implement it long after its flaws have become obvious. Comparing alternatives also makes it easier to articulate the trade-offs between different options. Successful organizations also use their condensed timeframes wisely as they consider their options. For example, one technique used is called 'consensus with qualification'. Issues and options are presented for the leadership team to consider, and they go round the table getting each person's perspective on the preferred course of action. Once these different perspectives have been shared, the group looks to see if there is consensus forming on the right course of action. If consensus emerges, the choice is made. However, if consensus is not forthcoming, the discussion and debate does not go on for long. The leader makes the decision. This leader, however, is making the decision having listened to the pros and cons from every angle. By creating a transparent decision-making process, where all of those at the table know their views have been heard (and can see that theirs is not the only perspective of relevance), there is more buy-in to the decision-making process and therefore greater chance of successful implementation. Another technique used by organizations in these environments is to stage their decision making. When there is rapid change and high levels of uncertainty, you want to leave yourself with options to evolve your response. Early decisions are coupled with defined timelines for when subsequent decisions will be made. By setting out a decision pathway, with established 'go'/'no go' decision points, means that stakeholders have surety over when a decision will be made, while retaining flexibility to adapt the strategy as a situation evolves.

57 Manage change carefully: Any changes in an organization's operation can introduce risk. How often does your organization make a change that introduces more issues than it solves? If the answer is 'often', you need a better operating discipline around change management. Get into the practice of undertaking a risk assessment whenever a major change is proposed. What could happen when we make this change? How will staff be affected? Will the change introduce other risks? Don't assume that you know what the implications of the change will be. Get into the habit of seeking others' perspectives. Run a five-minute online survey to get staff views on the proposed change and the possible positive and negative effects of it. Once your organization gets better at managing change, you will find that you can actually implement changes better and faster – improving your organization's agility.

58 Have good succession planning: Always look to the future. Who will be leading the organization in 5 or 10 years' time? Who will be running that critical process? Ensure that you have a 2IC (second in charge) or an 'apprentice' for all critical roles in your organization. Train these staff so that they are familiar with the role for when the key person moves on. This will also help when a crisis strikes and key personnel are unavailable.

59 Focus on knowledge transfer gaps: Organizations, especially big ones, are complex, with a lot of interdependencies. It can be hard to capture the knowledge and relationships that connect different parts of the organization. If you are documenting a certain process within your organization, include a section titled 'Interdependencies' which captures how this process connects with other processes in your organization. Create a mentoring programme to ensure that knowledge is shared across (and potentially between) organizations. Buddy senior and junior staff up, so that senior staff can coach junior staff on how the organization works. Mentoring is great, because it often captures the types of thing that can't be easily documented, such as people management skills, networking opportunities and organizational culture. Retired or retiring staff are also an invaluable resource. Consider phased retirement, so that they are actively involved in handing over to the next person taking over their role. During a crisis, retired staff may be willing to come back to lend a hand – so keep an up-to-date contact list for recent retirees. Run some crisis exercises with key people missing, to identify areas where you have remaining knowledge transfer gaps.

60 Encourage cross-department working: Promote opportunities for sharing and collaboration between departments. This could be as part of a crisis-planning day or perhaps as a workshop on a particularly challenging project or future challenge. On a planning day, get everyone to work out on whom they depend and who depends on them. Get them working in these groups to solve crisis scenarios. A cross-department group will tend to come up with more diverse and creative solutions. Also remember to communicate across silos. Make sure that everyone is aware of what is happening outside their department or team. Think about the best way to share this information. You could have an e-mailed newsletter, a video report, use Twitter or Facebook or have an intranet site. Make sure that the content is engaging and relevant so that it actually gets read. Also encourage people to move between silos by training them to work in more than one department. Get them to spend a day every month in another department to practise their skills. This will help to develop relationships across departments, increase staff skills, and help in a crisis when key personnel are unavailable; staff may also see things in other departments that could be used to make their part of the business even better. Make sure that each member of your staff is trained to do a number of roles and is flexible and willing to change roles in a crisis. Remember that crises often drain staff emotionally. If your staff are not used to stepping in to fill another person's shoes, they may find this difficult in a crisis. Develop this agility as part of your organization's culture.

61 Practise change: Staff who are used to, and accepting of, change will perform better when a disruption comes along. You want your staff to embrace change so much that they are disappointed when things remain the same! Change will liven up your work environment and keep minds fresh and innovative. So get practising now. Challenge your staff, every week for the next 12 weeks, to change just one thing they do in order to do their job better. Get them to note the changes down and discuss them with you. Don't forget to lead by example – change something yourself for this week and then let everyone know how it went. The change could be as simple as starting to recycle paper, having lunch with a new person at work, changing the way you deal with e-mail, or trying a new piece of technology or software.

62 Develop more flexible work practices: Review existing operating practices and see just how vulnerable they are to disruption. You don't want everything so efficient and finely tuned that the slightest deviation has the potential to bring your business down like a house of cards. Just-in-time practices are fine if you have the agility to adjust and adapt when there is disruption. Try mapping out your business workflow like a project Gantt chart and see what activities are on the critical path. Review how much time you have to get key parts of your business functioning again before disruption will start to spill over to other parts of your business. Look for ways to build in robustness, redundancy and flexibility to the way you operate. Don't be sucked in to thinking that resilience has to be expensive – in many cases, the additional investment required to deliver resilience is minimal. You might even discover new ways of doing things that save you money.

An ethos of resilience

You know you are doing well when resilience thinking and practice permeates everything your organization does:

63 Make resilience an organizational goal: While many people in your organization will implicitly understand that resilience is important for your organization, have you actually articulated it as an explicit goal for your organization? Make sure that everyone in the organization is aware of the importance of resilience and preparing themselves for the unexpected. Be intentional about driving a resilience agenda within your organization. Establish a group to develop a resilience strategy and enlist this group to be your champions for helping it to become a reality. If the term 'resilience' doesn't sit well for your organization, call it something different. Remember, the more you can align resilience with your organization's core objectives, the greater the chance of success.

64 Embed core values in day-to-day operations: Make sure that everything you and your staff do, including daily operations and interactions within your organization, reflects the core values of your business. If your operations and values don't match, you need to reassess either your values or your operations! Ask each staff member to state what your business is all about, or what the top priorities would be in a crisis. Do you get different answers? Perhaps they need to be reminded once again.

65 Build a culture of optimism: To be effective in a crisis you need to be optimistic, find fresh opportunities and believe that you will get through. When you have had a near-miss incident and are reviewing it, encourage everyone to say one positive thing or find a 'silver lining' about the event and how this will be good for the organization in the future.

66 Maintain a strategic focus: Don't ever become too complacent or comfortable. Annually review your operations and your organization's internal and external environment. Ask yourself: are we still meeting customer expectations? What are our competitors doing? Are there any upcoming regulatory changes that may impact our business? Are there new technologies that mean we could do things differently? Thinking ahead about where your organization is going is important for evolving your organization over the longer term. It also helps you to identify the things you might change immediately if the opportunity comes along. Crises present just such windows of opportunity for change.

As a final note, crises do not care what is on your desk at that moment. What was important a moment before, now isn't. You can't and won't be prepared for everything. Develop your management style so that you will cope when everything changes in an instant. Change and the unexpected are our reality. Don't fight it – find a way to work through it.

References and further reading

1 In particular, our core team within Resilient Organisations Ltd has played pivotal roles in the generation of many of these resilience ideas; see http://www. resorgs.org.nz/Our-People/resorgsltd.html

2 Resilience HealthCheck Tool – for more information see: http://www. organisationalresilience.gov.au/HealthCheck/Pages/default.aspx

3 Resilience Thumbprint Tool – for more information see: http://www.resorgs.org. nz/Resources/resilience-thumbprint-tool.html

4 Resilience Benchmark Tool – for more information see: http://www.resorgs.org. nz/benchmark-resilience-tool.html

5 Vargo, J, Sullivan, J and Parsons, D (2013) *Benchmarking Resilience: Organisational resilience in the Australian water industry*, Resilient Organisations, http://www.resorgs.org.nz/images/stories/pdfs/OrganisationalResilience/sw_ resilience_scorecard.pdf

6 Brown, C, Seville, E and Vargo J (2014) *Bay of Plenty Lifelines Group Resilience Benchmark Report*, Resilient Organisations Research Report 2014/06, September, http://www.resorgs.org.nz/images/stories/pdfs/bay_of_ plenty_resilience_benchmark_report.pdf

7 Parson, D, Hatton, T, Seville, E *et al* (2014) *Chaos to Teamwork – A leader's role in crisis*, Resilient Organisations Business Resource 2014/C, ISSN 2381-9790 (Print), ISSN 2381-9804 (Online), http://www.resorgs.org.nz/chaos-to-teamwork.html

8 Parsons, D (2014) *Adversity Leadership*, Resilience Expert Advisory Group, Australian Attorney General's Department, http://www.organisationalresilience. gov.au/resources/Documents/AdversityLeadership.pdf

9 Tools for developing employee engagement surveys – see: https://www. surveymonkey.com/mp/employee-engagement-survey/

10 The Wellbeing Game – for more information see: http://thewellbeinggame.org. nz/home/how

11 Employee Resilience Tool – for more information see: http://www.resorgs.org. nz/Resources/employee-resilience-tool.html

12 Design thinking Bootcamp Bootleg – for more information see: http://dschool. stanford.edu/use-our-methods/

13 Organizational learning:

– Garvin, DA, Edmondson, AC and Gino, F (2008) Is yours a learning organization? *Harvard Business Review*, **86** (3), p 109, https://hbr.org/2008/03/is-yours-a-learning-organization

– Diagnostic Organizational Learning tool – for more information see: http://los.hbs.edu

14 Baird, L, Holland, P and Deacon, S (1999) Learning from action: imbedding more learning into the performance fast enough to make a difference, *Organizational Dynamics*, **27** (4), pp 19–31

15 ISO standards for risk and business continuity management:

– ISO 31000:2009, *Risk management*, http://www.iso.org/iso/home/standards/iso31000.htm

– ISO 22313:2012 *Societal security – Business continuity management systems – Requirements*, http://www.iso.org/iso/home/store/catalogue_tc/catalogue_detail.htm?csnumber=50038

16 Resilience Quick Start Guides for printing out: http://resorgs.org.nz/resilience-quickstart-guides

17 Ahmad, R, Hatton, T, Seville, E *et al* (2015) *First Aid for Business: In the midst of a crisis?* Resilient Organisations Business Resource 2015A, ISSN 2381-9790 (Print), ISSN 2381-9804 (Online), http://www.resorgs.org.nz/first-aid-business.html

18 Parsons, D (2014) *Adversity Leadership*, Resilience Expert Advisory Group, Australian Attorney General's Department, http://www.organisationalresilience.gov.au/resources/Documents/AdversityLeadership.pdf

19 Walker, B, Fraser, M and Nilakant, V (2014) *Staffed or Stuffed: Creating resilience through your people*, Resilient Organisations Business Resource 2014/A, ISSN 2381-9790, http://www.resorgs.org.nz/staffed-or-stuffed.html

20 Brown, C, Vargo, J, Seville, E *et al* (2015) *Cover Your Assets: A short guide to selecting and getting the best from your commercial insurance policy*, Resilient Organisations Business Resource 2014/B, ISSN 2381-9790 (Print), ISSN 2381-9804 (Online), http://www.resorgs.org.nz/cover-your-assets.html

21 Decision making in high-velocity environments:

– Eisenhardt, KM (2008) Speed and strategic choice: how managers accelerate decision making, *California Management Review*, **50** (2), pp 102–16

– Eisenhardt, KM (1999) Strategy as strategic decision making, *Sloan Management Review*, **40** (3), pp 65–72

– Eisenhardt, KM (1989) Making fast strategic decisions in high-velocity environments, *The Academy of Management Journal*, **32** (3), pp 543–76

– Clark, K and Collins, C (2002) Strategic decision-making in high velocity environments: a theory revisited and a test, in *Creating Value: Winners in the new business environment*, ed MA Hitt, R Amit, CE Lucier *et al*, pp 213–39, Blackwell, Oxford

INDEX